SOUTH BEACH
The Delaplaine 2021 Long Weekend Guide

Andrew Delaplaine

NO BUSINESS HAS PAID A SINGLE PENNY OR GIVEN _ANYTHING_ TO BE INCLUDED IN THIS BOOK.

Senior Editors - *Renee & Sophie Delaplaine*
Senior Writer - **James Cubby**

Gramercy Park Press
New York – London – Paris

WANT 3 **FREE** THRILLERS?
Why, of course you do!

If you like these writers--
Vince Flynn, Brad Thor, Tom Clancy, James Patterson, David Baldacci, John Grisham, Brad Meltzer, Daniel Silva, Don DeLillo
If you like these TV series –
House of Cards, Scandal, West Wing, The Good Wife, Madam Secretary, Designated Survivor

---

You'll love the **unputdownable** series about Jack's world, with political intrigue, romance, suspense.

Besides writing travel books, I've written political thrillers for many years that have delighted hundreds of thousands of readers. I want to introduce you to my work!
Send me an email and I'll send you a link where you can download the first 3 books in my bestselling series, absolutely FREE.
Tell me you're responding to my offer in this book.

andrewdelaplaine@mac.com

MIAMI &
SOUTH BEACH
The Delaplaine
Long Weekend Guide

TABLE OF CONTENTS

CORAL GABLES
COCONUT GROVE
KEY BISCAYNE

5

CHAPTER 1

By Way of Introduction – Why Miami? Transportation & Tips for Getting Around - Parking Headaches - If Your Car Is Towed - The Best Cab Company - Specific Information During Your Visit - Visitors' Centers

BY WAY OF INTRODUCTION

Food, Wine & Travel

I've written about food, wine and travel for decades, and while I've lived on South Beach since the late-1980s, most of the writing about food and wine had to do with New York or London or Paris, definitely *not* South Beach. One could write endless "travel" pieces about Miami, but the "food" and "wine" offerings were pretty much limited unless you went to **Joe's Stone Crab** for the food and **The Forge** for the wine.

My, my ... how things have changed.

Miami and South Beach are now year-round destinations. The nightlife industry, the fuel that drives the engine, churns all through the summer, never letting up. Most of the top bars and clubs have licenses that permit them to remain open selling liquor till 5am.

As a butler I once had in London used to say: *Raathuur!*

Chefs from all over the world have established outposts on South Beach, eager to be part of the scene.

Boutique hotels (the **W**, the **Setai**, the **Gale**, etc.) have flooded in and cranked up the quality of service to the 4- and even 5-Star levels. (Trust me, child, it wasn't always like this.)

This really is a world-class town. And in this book I will share some things I like about it (and a few I don't.) This is not a book to tell you how to get from your hometown to Miami International Airport, or from MIA to South Beach. You can figure that out by yourself. (And if you can't, stay home.)

It's also *not a comprehensive book* covering the County. It's not a phone book or something purporting to cover everything. God forbid. Who'd want to read such a book? No. This, like my other *Guides*, is my *personal* take on the scene for visitors, not necessarily residents. Thus, there are no listings for some of the great restaurants I've trekked to in South and West Miami. The listings are intentionally brief, so they can be digested fast.

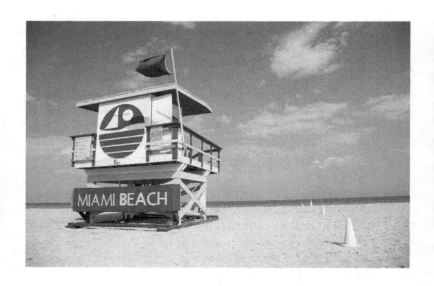

WHY MIAMI?

Because it may be the most *interesting* city in the U.S.
There are probably only a handful of cities in America that
offer truly distinctive "feels," and by that I mean a unique
sensation you get when you're there that you don't get
anywhere else.

Boston has it, Charleston has it, New York, San
Francisco, New Orleans, Chicago, Vegas and a handful of
other cities large and small have it. But, to be honest, if
you removed my blindfold on a street in Buffalo or
Cleveland, I'd have a hard time telling them apart at first
glance. (Or even second glance.)

Not so Miami.

And it's not all sex, drugs and rock 'n roll. (Well ... it's
not, really.) It's home to some major league cultural
institutions, from the **Miami City Ballet** headed by
Edward Villella; the **New World Symphony** with topper
Michael Tilson Thomas, the stupendously successful **Art**

Basel. The off-the-wall collection of tens of thousands of items of decorative and propaganda art assembled by Mickey Wolfson in his **Wolfsonian Museum** now operated by FIU is worth a trip to Miami all by itself. As is the **South Beach Wine & Food Festival** pushed to the top of the heap in its category by the relentless energy of **Lee Brian Schrager.** Schrager and the others have an infectious optimism that has transformed small start-ups into world-class institutions that have made lasting contributions in their fields.

As a young city, these institutions were founded and nurtured by strong-willed individuals. And built from the ground up. If they began with something to prove, they proved it.

But I'm assuming you know why you're coming here. I'm not here to sell you on the town. If it's February, it's probably got a lot more to do with a suntan than with Schumann, and you're probably more interested in a good mojito than Mozart. And you might not care or even know the difference between a Degas and a Duchamp, a Picasso and a Pissarro. And maybe you *are* here because of the sex, drugs and rock 'n roll. Whatever.

Let's face it: how many towns in America let their clubs, bars and dives stay open till 5am selling booze? (And everything else—they don't call it Sodom by the Sea for nuttin'!)

Miami has an edge. And the edge is what's most interesting about it, with the hundred different ethnic influences all mixing together to make it so dramatic, Mozart and the ballet notwithstanding.

TIPS FOR GETTING AROUND

AIRPORT FLYER
http://www.miamidade.gov/transit/routes_detail.asp?route=150

One of the most economical ways to get to the Miami Airport is to take the Airport Flyer, an express bus with service between MIA, Metrorail, and Miami Beach that costs only a few dollars. The Airport Flyer runs every half hour from 6 a.m. to 11 p.m. Look for the Airport Flyer signs at bus stops.

SOUTH BEACH LOCAL BUS
This local shuttle service is the cheapest way to get around South Beach. It stops every 10 or 15 minutes at numerous corners. It's air-conditioned and only costs 25 cents. (You'll see signs posted everywhere.) Personally, I use Uber to get around, but if I needed to or had a budget, I'd use this service religiously.

MIAMI HOP-ON HOP-OFF BUS
https://city-sightseeing.com
Visitors to Miami can travel all over Miami and learn about the city at the same time on one of the many red double-decker Hop-On Hop-Off Buses. Buses travel to Downtown Miami, the Design District, Coconut Grove, Coral Gables and beyond. A two-day pass costs $39 allowing you to hop on and hop off at any stop as many times as you wish. For schedules and list of stops.

BIKES
MIAMI HOP-ON HOP-OFF BUS
https://city-sightseeing.com
Visitors to Miami can travel all over Miami and learn about the city at the same time on one of the many red double-decker Hop-On Hop-Off Buses. Buses travel to Downtown Miami, the Design District, Coconut Grove, Coral Gables and beyond. A two-day pass costs $39 allowing you to hop on and hop off at any stop as many times as you wish. For schedules and list of stops.

MIAMI HOP-ON HOP-OFF BUS
https://city-sightseeing.com
Visitors to Miami can travel all over Miami and learn
about the city at the same time on one of the many red
double-decker Hop-On Hop-Off Buses. Buses travel to
Downtown Miami, the Design District, Coconut Grove,
Coral Gables and beyond. A two-day pass costs $39
allowing you to hop on and hop off at any stop as many
times as you wish. For schedules and list of stops.

BIKES
https://citibikemiami.com
Since most of South Beach is located within one square
mile you'll see locals getting around by skateboard and
bicycles. Biking is a viable means of transportation in
Miami Beach and there are bicycle stands all over the
beach and many well-marked bike lanes. Citi bike, a
popular bike sharing system that has partnered with the
City of Miami Beach, offers approximately 1,000 bikes
accessible from 100 stations located throughout Miami
Beach. This system allows renters to pick up a bike (a
charge card is needed) and the bike can be returned to any
of the 100 stations located throughout Miami Beach.

RENTING A CAR? THINK TWICE
We recommend you rent a car only if you're planning on
leaving South Beach a lot. Parking is a never-ending
hassle, the City writes tickets relentlessly and ruthlessly
and just finding parking spots on the weekends is a major
pain in the ass.

Since South Beach is so small, we suggest you leave
your car parked securely in a city-owned garage and either
walk or take short Uber / Lyft rides. Even if you use the
valet service when you go to a fancy hotel for a drink, the
valet will cost you between $30 and $40.

11

The valets at restaurants are often *not* a real convenience. When it's busy, it can take quite a bit of time for the valet to retrieve your car. So best advice: Uber / Lyft it everywhere. I live here, and I do.

IF YOUR CAR IS TOWED
And trust me, it *will* be towed if you park in a tow away zone. Towing is a cottage industry in this town. The problem: you won't notice the signs until it's too late. Some businesses watch the often hard-to-see tow away zones very carefully and spy as you park in what will look like an OK place, but is really a tow away zone, and within seconds of you leaving your car, a call is made and you are towed.

The towing companies (there are two of them that have a monopoly) make hundreds of thousands of dollars each year on unsuspecting tourists. The City even gets a kickback (uh, I'm sorry, an "administrative fee") for each car towed. It's a shame, but it's true. In other towns, a tow truck can be thought of as providing a service. Here, it's a predatory act sanctioned by the City to rip you off. So, you've been warned.

When your car is towed, it won't be far away. It will be over on a little street just a few minutes from Lincoln Road on the way to the Venetian Causeway. When you get back to where you left your car, look for the little green sign (that you didn't notice before) posted on a wall and this sign will tell you which company has your car. Call **Tremont Towing, 305-672-2395**, or **Beach Towing, 305-534-2128**, to find out which one has your car and how much it is (it'll be between $100 and $350, depending on the season). Summon **UBER,** and go get your car. Stop by an ATM machine. The buggers only take cash, of course.

Speaking of **UBER**. The absolute best way to enjoy South Beach if you are driving over in your own car or a rental is to park the car in a garage (like the one centrally located just north of Lincoln Road on 17th Street), leave it there and take **UBER.** This is what I do. I leave my car parked in front of my house, especially after 6 or 7 in the evening when it's hard to find a good space and then I take UBER all over town.

You'll ride in nicer cars for cheaper fares and there's no tipping. If you don't have the Uber app, download it now on your smartphone and use my code when you sign up and get a couple of free rides. Code is – **Andrewd145**

THE BEST CAB COMPANY (There Isn't One)
Central Cab – 305-532-5555 – is a company based on South Beach, so their drivers always know the best route to take you anywhere. It's not the "best" cab company. It's the "only" cab company. I haven't used these old, smelly beat-up cabs in years, not since **Uber / Lyft** got started. Everywhere you're going is only five or six minutes away on the island. Use my Uber code if you do not have the app and you'll get a couple of free rides. Cheaper than a cab by far. Code is – **Andrewd145**

SPECIFIC INFO DURING YOUR VISIT
Check out the listings in the weekly newspaper New Times, which has boxes on every corner, or use your laptop (or increasingly these days, even your cell phone) and go to their web site, www.miaminewtimes.com. The Miami Herald only has a good list in its Friday edition. But they also have comprehensive listings online at www.miamiherald.com.

VISITORS' CENTERS

THE ART DECO WELCOME CENTER
1001 Ocean Drive, Miami Beach, (10th and Ocean), 305-763-8026
www.mdpl.org/welcome-center/visitors-center/

Located on Ocean Drive across from the beach, the Art Deco Welcome Center offers visitors a center for information, tours, and a gift shop filled with Miami Beach memorabilia and souvenirs as well as Art Deco gifts and books.

ART DECO TOURS
Learn all about South Beach's historical Art Deco District in a VIP Art Deco Walking Tour. Transport in time back to the 20's, 30's and beyond. Learn about the colorful history and admire unique architecture and design with exclusive access to interiors and rooftops. Elevate the experience with the Art Deco Cocktail tour. For schedule and rates, visit www.artdecotours.com or call 305-814-4058.

MIAMI BEACH VISITORS' CENTER (MBVC) AT THE CONVENTION CENTER
530 17TH ST, Miami Beach. 305-672-1270. Daily from 10-4.
WEB: www.miamibeachguest.com.
This state-of-the-art facility offers a multilingual staff along with tourist, business and residential amenities. Their literature rack holds over 200 brochures, magazines, newspapers and maps, calendar of events and visitors' guides full of helpful facts. They offer on-the-spot hotel accommodations, and **20 daily tour excursions.** They are the official distributor of Miami's best attraction pass, the Go Miami Card. They provide the MB chamber of commerce's newest feature, the In Card, which offers tourists and residents money-saving amenities at local businesses. Hotel reservations: 800-666-4519.

MIAMI BEACH LATIN CHAMBER OF COMMERCE & VISITORS' CENTER
1620 Drexel Ave / 305-641-1414.

WEB: www.miamibeach.org
Located on the grounds of the 1920 Community Church
(worth a stop just to see the church) on Lincoln Road.

MIAMI BEACH GAY & LESBIAN CHAMBER OF COMMERCE
1130 Washington Avenue – First Floor North / 305-673-4440.
WEB: www.gogaymiami.com - In the Old City Hall
Building.

CHAPTER 2
LODGING

SOUTH BEACH
(The High Life – The Middle Ground - Cheaper Alternatives)

MIDDLE BEACH / NORTH BEACH

DOWNTOWN / BRICKELL

COCONUT GROVE

KEY BISCAYNE

CORAL GABLES

* * *

SOUTH BEACH

The High Life – The Middle Ground
Cheaper Alternatives

I'll say right off that my favorite hotel is the **Raleigh.**
Sure, sometimes the upholstery will be flawed, or there is
a leaky faucet. But for an Art Deco hotel, you can't beat it.
Former Ocean Drive Managing Editor Eric Newill and I
have spent many an hour in the little bar off the lobby, and
it's still my favorite "small" bar in a town with a lot of big,
nasty, noisy ones.

My second favorite is the **Delano** because... it's just such a
scene. Exquisitely conceived and usually run pretty well,
too.

I like the **Betsy** on Ocean Drive, just off a complete
makeover. And they have owners who really care. They
are not trying to fool you. Beautifully done. **Dream**,
tucked away down on an unfortunate sad part of Collins
Avenue, is also very good.

If I wanted a newer, more modern place, I'd splurge for
the **Setai**. But then I'd probably never leave the place once
I checked in, so what's the point?

1 HOTEL SOUTH BEACH
2341 Collins Ave, Miami Beach, 305-604-1000
www.1hotels.com
Newly opened upscale beachfront hotel (formerly the
Gansevoort and also the Perry) with 4 outdoor pools

including rooftop lounge/pool offering an incredible ocean view. After the $100 million they plowed into this huge resort, one hopes it keeps the same name for more than a year or two. Accommodations are top-notch with sophisticated rooms featuring driftwood on the walls. Amenities include: Complimentary Wi-Fi, 55-inch flat-screen TVs and Nespresso machines. Hotel features high-end restaurant, rooftop bar, fitness center, and direct beach access.

AC HOTEL MIAMI BEACH
2912 Collins Ave, Miami Beach, 786-264-4720
www.marriott.com/hotels/travel/miaac-ac-hotel-miami-beach
Located a bit north of South Beach, this hotel, like so many South Beach hotels, offers a great lounge with a happening bar scene. Bar offers a menu of local craft beer, wine on tap, creative cocktails and a bar menu of curated tapas.

BENTLEY HOTEL
510 Ocean Dr., Miami Beach: 305-538-1700
www.thebentleyhotel.com
Nice enough property, but it's on the busiest corner you can imagine where every car coming off the Causeway turns onto Ocean Drive.

CATALINA
1732-1756 Collins Ave., Miami Beach: 305-674-1160.
www.catalinahotel.com.
The owners have cobbled together three buildings on bustling Collins Avenue to form the Catalina. Cheap rooms, but nicely maintained. Always busy. Has a happening restaurant and bar scene as well.

CHELSEA

944 Washington Ave., Miami Beach: 305-534-4069
www.thehotelchelsea.com
Has a nice restaurant and cozy bar, across from the
Wolfsonian Museum. Rooms are spotless the two times I
was in them, staff friendly.

CHESTERFIELD HOTEL & SUITES

855 Collins Ave., Miami Beach: 305-531-5831
www.thechesterfieldhotel.com
Art Deco-design hotel has been completely renovated to
modern standards. Animal prints abound in a funky South
Beach style that fills the hotel. Complimentary transfers to
and from the airport.

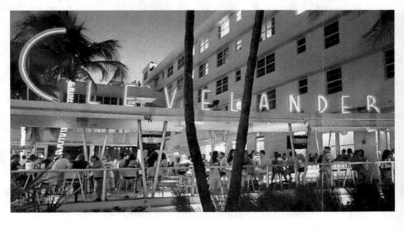

CLEVELANDER HOTEL

1020 Ocean Dr., Miami Beach: 877-532-4006
www.clevelander.com
Has 60 revamped rooms and ROCKSTAR Suites, two
rooftop decks with ocean-front and city views, enhanced
poolside bars, and a new café-style menu. The 1937 art
deco landmark famous for its fun parties, year-round is
back stronger than ever showcasing the hottest DJ's,

bands, dancers, musicians, models and performance groups. Gets rowdy on weekends.

DELANO
1685 Collins Ave., Miami Beach: 305-672-2000.
www.delano-hotel.com
Can't say enough about the place. Love it to stay in. Love it for breakfast. Love it for drinks. Love it for lunch. Love it at night. Right on the beach.

DREAM SOUTH BEACH
1111 Collins Ave, Miami Beach, 305-673-4747
www.dreamhotels.com
The Dream South Beach is a mixture of Art Deco style with modern design as this hotel has joined two iconic Art Deco hotels, the Tudor and the Palmer, to create this new modern complex that feature a rooftop pool. Just a block from the white sand beach and next door to Villa by Barton G, also known as the famed Versace Mansion. This hotel boasts 108 guestrooms and suites featuring modern amenities including large flat screen TVs, high-speed Wi-

Fi (for a fee), Etro bath amenities and onsite restaurant and rooftop lounge. Conveniently located near museums, restaurants, shopping, and attractions like the New World Center, the Fillmore Miami Beach, and the Art Deco Welcome Center.

ESSEX HOUSE
1001 Collins Ave., Miami Beach: 877-532-4006
https://www.essexhotel.com/
This property is in a very busy part of Collins Avenue that's a bit much for me. But this property is a good bargain. Also, even if you don't stay here, slip into the lobby for a look at its Art Deco lobby that has some unusual Egyptian motifs that will have you scratching your head.

GALE SOUTH BEACH & REGENT HOTEL
1690 Collins Ave., Miami Beach: 305-673-0199
www.galehotel.com

Two 1940s Art Deco hotels connected and beautifully refurbished. Boutique atmosphere with 87 guest rooms, great location near the beach. $$$

HILTON BENTLEY
101 Ocean Dr., Miami Beach: 305-938-4600
www.hiltonbentleymiami.com
AAA 4-Diamond hotel, not to be confused with the Bentley on Fifth Street 4 blocks down in quiet SoFi. Each suite has been meticulously designed, fully equipped with 42-inch LCD televisions, stainless steel gourmet kitchenettes, and featuring majestic views of the ocean and Miami Beach. Has Spa 101, as well as the great **Prime Italian** and **Bentley Beach Club**.

THE HOTEL
801 Collins Ave., Miami Beach: 305-531-2222.
www.thehotelofsouthbeach.com.
This used to be called The Tiffany, and is now called, simply, The Hotel. Totally redesigned (almost reconceived) by **Todd Oldham**, from the lobby to the expertly refurbished rooms.

HYATT CENTRIC SOUTH BEACH MIAMI
1600 Collins Ave, Miami Beach, 305-428-1234
https://southbeachmiami.centric.hyatt.com/en/hotel/
Hyatt brings its contemporary lifestyle brand to this newly built 10-story glass-tower hotel featuring 105 modern guest rooms. Amenities include: complimentary Wi-Fi and flat-screen TVs. rooftop deck, and fitness center. Hotel features include: Spanish-Mediterranean eatery, rooftop deck, and fitness center. Smoke-free hotel.

LENNOX HOTEL
1900 Collins Ave, Miami Beach, 305-531-6800
www.lennoxmiamibeach.com

NEIGHBORHOOD: South Beach

The former 1936 Peter Miller Hotel has been renovated (to the tune of over $100 million), maintaining the original Art Deco and Mediterranean exterior, into this first-class luxury hotel with over 100 modern guestrooms, 13 with balconies. The rooms feature handcrafted furnishings from Patagonia, natural elements and eco-friendly and upcycled materials meticulously curated by acclaimed Argentinian interior designer Juan Ciavarella. Amenities - curated minibars with Nosh MARKT products, complimentary Wi-Fi, and flat-screen TVs. Hotel facilities include a high-end chic restaurant, comfortable lounge, a Mediterranean-inspired courtyard with a pool, a bar and a terrace. Located one-block from the beach, where the hotel maintains a private beach area with lounge chairs, umbrellas and towels. Near restaurants, bars, and museums. Non-smoking hotel.

LOEWS
1601 Collins Ave., Miami Beach: 305-604-1601
www.loewshotels.com
Standard issue modern hotel. No real character. The 10 or 15 different design elements they threw together in the lobby makes the place look like the inside of a goat's stomach. Somebody was high.

LORD BALFOUR SOUTH BEACH
350 Ocean Dr., Miami Beach; 855-269-2426
www.lordbalfourmiami.com
Formerly the Wave Hotel, this 64-room 1940 hotel has been transformed into an art-filled boutique hotel. Attracting the hip and trendy crowd, the hotel amenities include: complimentary Wi-Fi, 40" HD TVs and IPod/iPhone with alarm clock. Located south of historic district but close to clubs/restaurants like Nikki Beach and Prime 112.

MARRIOTT STANTON
161 Ocean Dr., Miami Beach: 305-536-7700
www.miamibeachmarriott.com
This deluxe oceanfront Art Deco hotel is located on Ocean
Drive down in SoFi (South of Fifth), the more civilized
part of Ocean Drive. Anywhere north of Fifth Street is a
zoo. Balconies with magnificent views. Starbucks and
Deco Blue Bar located on-site as well as a great restaurant.

METROPOLITAN BY COMO, MIAMI BEACH
2445 Collins Ave., Miami Beach; 305-695-3600
www.comohotels.com/metropolitanmiamibeach
This rebuilt Art Deco hotel – the former Traymore Hotel –
with a new look and brand (COMO has locations in
London, Bangkok, Maldives and Turks & Caicos). The
newly opened 74-room hotel is located in the heart of
Miami Beach historic district and offers modern luxury.
Guests can enjoy complimentary Wi-Fi, swimming pool,
24-hour fitness center and on-site Traymore restaurant.

MONDRIAN
1100 West Ave., Miami Beach: 305-514-1500
www.mondrian-miami.com
Now this place has got to be seen – the interior is stunning,
but it's still copycat **Delano**-esque with its use of white.
(The same company owns this property.) Unlike any of the
other hotels on my list, this one is located on West Avenue
overlooking the Bay, so you get a stunning sunset every
day.

NAUTILUS
1825 Collins Ave, Miami Beach, 305-503-5700
www.arlohotels.com
This hotel was originally designed by the famed architect
Morris Lapidus (known more for the Fontainebleau and

the Eden Roc further up Collins Avenue, whose lobbies, by the way, you really ought to make a special trip to see), this place has been updated and redesigned as an upscale property featuring 250 elegant guestrooms including 51 suites and a two-bedroom Penthouse. A couple of Lapidus features are preserved in the 25-foot high lobby—the sunken bar, very 1950s, and the "stairway to nowhere." Lapidus often installed a flight of stairs in his lobbies, even if when you got to the top of the stairs there was only a wall. Amenities include: balconies, flat-screen TVs, and complimentary Wi-Fi. The hotel is located 650 feet from the beach and features a salt-water pool flanked by cabanas, day-beds and a nice poolside bar; sun terrace; live entertainment; on-site chef-driven dining and a lounge that attracts not only me, but a hip crowd as well. (I'm the one in the corner.)

OCEAN FIVE HOTEL
436 Ocean Dr., Miami Beach: 305-532-7093
www.oceanfive.com
This unpretentious boutique hotel is down in the tranquil SoFi (South of Fifth).

THE PELICAN
826 Ocean Dr., Miami Beach: 305-673-3373.
www.pelicanhotel.com.
While it took Diesel Jeans owner Renzo Rosso until 1996 to finally open a store on Lexington Avenue in New York, he has been on South Beach much longer, buying this hotel in the early '90s, as I vaguely recall. There's a huge penthouse suite with a Jacuzzi where I've been to many parties. Each room has a kind of wacky theme to it, and this is about the *least* Art Deco-y hotel on South Beach. But it sure is fun.

PRIME HOTEL
100 Ocean Dr., Miami Beach: 305-532-0553
www.primehotel-miami.com
This 14-room boutique hotel is located where the trendy
restaurant **Prime 112** is. Has a stunning rooftop pool,
state-of-the-art in-room entertainment, and luxurious
furnishings and bathrooms. Very *luxe.*

RALEIGH (Closed for Renovations at press time)
1775 Collins Ave., Miami Beach: 305-534-6300
www.raleighhotel.com/
My favorite hotel on South Beach. I've been haunting its
intimate lobby bar ever since Ken Zarrilli bought the
property (in 1991, if memory serves) and began the
laborious process of restoring it. He sold out for millions
to Andre Balazs, and he sold it in 2010 (He still owns the
Standard over on the Venetian Causeway.). A Japanese
concern bought it, and now it's owned by designer Tommy
Hilfiger. We're all scared to death what he's going to do to
"improve" the property, but for now, it's still quite special.
There's a certain something about this place that when you
walk into the lobby, you really feel as if you've been
transported back to the 1940s. It's a fleeting sensation, of

course, that only lasts for a minute or so, but it's the only place on South Beach where you'll get it at all. Do yourself a favor and walk around the pool—it's the most striking pool in the whole town and deserves to be seen.

THE REDBURY SOUTH BEACH
1776 Collins Ave., Miami Beach; 305-604-1776
www.theredbury.com/southbeach
This rebirth of the former Fairfax hotel which sat vacant for years has now been transformed into a hip new 69-room boutique hotel. Named after its hot sister location in Hollywood, Calif, this new venue boasts a rock and roll theme mixed with old school Miami Beach glamor. Checkout the scene around the rooftop pool and taste the delicious handmade pasta, pizza, and other Italian favorites from James Beard Award-winning chef Tony Mantuano in the on-site eatery Lorenzo. Guests are granted access to the Raleigh Hotel's beach and SLS Hotel's fitness facilities.

RICHMOND HOTEL
1757 Collins Ave., Miami Beach: 305-538-1411
www.richmondhotel.com
Designed in the early 1940s by L. Murray Dixon, this oceanfront Art Deco masterpiece offers luxurious accommodations with state-of-the-art amenities. Relax on the stunning pool deck or in the coconut palm tropical garden, or take a few steps onto the white sandy beach. Experience the charm and energy of South Beach while staying at this private, secluded and elegant hotel.

RIVIERA
318 20th St., Miami Beach: 305 538-7444
www.rivierahotelsouthbeach.com/
A few blocks from Lincoln Road and a couple of blocks from the ocean.

SAGAMORE

1671 Collins Ave., Miami Beach: 305-535-8088
www.sagamoresouthbeach.com
I just love the name "Sagamore." Always have. Back in
the late '80s, I used to eat cheap chicken wings and gulp
down cold oysters by the dozen at the tacky tiki hut
overlooking the ocean by the two swimming pools (one
had salt water, one had fresh). The place was full of poor
people and deadbeats. Nowadays, the poor people are gone
(along with the tiki hut, the salt water pool, the superior
chicken wings and the low prices), but it's a gorgeous
place.

SEAGULL HOTEL MIAMI BEACH

100 21st St., Miami Beach: 305-538-6631
www.seagullhotelmiamibeach.com/
Directly on the beach with sweeping views of the Atlantic.
It is a cozy, tropical hotel with exotic murals and oversized
rattan furniture. All nonsmoking guest rooms with free
Wi-Fi. Within walking distance of Lincoln Road.

SETAI

2001 Collins Ave., Miami Beach: 305-520-6000
www.thesetaihotel.com
Ultimate in luxury. The only thing I don't like about the
Setai is that they've created such an enclosed environment
that you don't really feel like you're on South Beach at all.
Their lavish Sunday brunch is perhaps the most expensive
one in town. But it's HUGE. Don't plan on eating for a
day ahead or a day after you slog through this food-fest.

SHORE CLUB

1901 Collins Ave., Miami Beach: 305-695-3100
www.shoreclub.com
Was a hot spot till it was eclipsed by the **W** and the **Gale**.
Owned by the same company that owns the **Delano** and

the **Mondrian** over on West Avenue, so everything's really quite tip-top. There's a lot of activity here at night, what with the trendy **Skybar** packing 'em in.

SLS HOTEL SOUTH BEACH
1701 Collins Ave., Miami Beach: 305-674-1701
www.slshotels.com/southbeach
Elegant, chic newly refurbished luxury hotel with an incredibly unimaginative name. SLS? Who came up with that? But it's a hotbed of hip activity. A **Philippe Starck** creation with assistance from names like **Lenny Kravitz.** Beautiful hotel & two pools with top-notch restaurants. $$$$

SOUTH SEAS HOTEL
1751 Collins Ave., Miami Beach: 305-538-1411
www.southseashotel.com
Excellent location right in the middle of the action. Nothing fancy.

THE STANDARD
40 Island Ave., Miami Beach: 305-673-1717
www.standardhotels.com
With so many of the first class hotels offering spas, there's no real reason to come off South Beach (this place is located on the first island of the Venetian Causeway, just over a short bridge from South Beach). But it is on the water on Biscayne Bay, and that makes it very nice. Another good thing about it is that it IS off South Beach, and quiet at night, so you don't have any of the noise and nonsense and kids throwing beer bottles at each other when they pour out of the clubs at 3 or 4 a.m. Owned by Andre Balazs, who sold the Raleigh in 2010 but in his grand hotel empire decided to keep this nice and subdued place on South Beach.

VICTOR

1144 Ocean Dr., Miami Beach: 305-779-8700
www.hotelvictorsouthbeach.com
Of the three hotels I list on Ocean Drive, this is the
trendiest, hippest. DJs playing on weekend, lots of parties.
A gorgeously restored Art Deco gem. When you're in the
lobby, you feel like you're on an ocean liner in the 1930s.
Second story pool deck lots of fun.

W SOUTH BEACH

2201 Collins Ave., Miami Beach: 305-938-3000
www.wsouthbeach.com
What can I say that other people haven't said? They spared
no expense, and it's clear they want you to notice it. A
little pretentious in that sense. Here, don't forget, you have
one of the hippest scenes playing out in all its shallowness
on South Beach right now: you have **Mr. Chow**. You have
the **Club Wall** (with only table service, it's a real
"experience" watching the chemistry of young girls circle
the moneyed bozos at the tables). But the rooms are
lovely, the service so-so. It can be flawless one day, and
then the very next day, totally crummy.

WINTER HAVEN

1400 Ocean Dr., Miami Beach: 305-531-5571
www.winterhavenhotelsobe.com
71 welcoming guest rooms. Hotel offers a variety of ocean
views, an Ocean Drive patio and Martini bar, daily
breakfast, Wi-Fi throughout, beach towels and chairs,
multilingual staff, rooftop sundeck, and use of the pool at
the sister Blue Moon Hotel.

Z OCEAN

1437 Collins Ave., Miami Beach: 305-672-4554
www.zoceanhotelsouthbeach.com
Nestled on the north end of world-famous Ocean Drive,
this hotel offers a chic and intimate haven, as well as
access to vibrant, see-and-be-seen nightlife. The suites
feature luxurious California King size beds complemented
by a memorable walk-in shower experience. Oversized
private terraces provide the perfect setting to enjoy the
hustle and bustle of South Beach. The hotel is an intimate
affair, offering impeccable service, quality and location
right on Miami Beach.

MIDDLE BEACH / NORTH BEACH

MIDDLE MIAMI BEACH

All these hotels share one thing in common: they're NOT
on South Beach. So if it's a more tranquil environment
you're looking for, this is the place to stay. You're only 5
or 10 minutes (depending on traffic) from South Beach by
Uber. Use my code when signing up for the app – you'll
get a couple of free rides, and so will I. Code is –
Andrewd145

CIRCA39 HOTEL

3900 Collins Ave., Miami Beach: 305-538-4900
www.circa39.com
Recently renovated. Has a nice eatery on site, Jules
Kitchen.

CASA FAENA
3500 Collins Ave., Miami Beach: 305-604-8485
www.faena.com/Casa-Faena/
Originally built in 1928, this has been recently restored.
Has volcanic rock columns, Spanish Colonial art, and an
in-lobby splash spa. Rooms and suites overlook an interior
courtyard. Italian restaurant on site.

CONFIDANTE
4041 Collins Ave, Miami Beach, 305-424-1234
http://theconfidante.unbound.hyatt.com/en/hotel/home.htm
l
One of Miami's newest hotels to open after an $80 million
renovation, this unique hotel constructed from three towers
of different eras – one a 1940s Art Deco skyscraper—
features 380 beautifully decorated rooms. It's one of those
places up in Mid Beach that puts it out of everything
happening on South Beach, so be sure you know where
this place is located before booking. (Me? I'd stay on
South Beach and take Uber up here to hang out in the
lobby) Amenities include: complimentary Wi-Fi, flat-
screen TVs and minibars. Hotel features include a library-
like cocktail lounge, two heated pools, an open-air spa,
and a fitness center.

COURTYARD BY MARRIOTT
3925 Collins Ave., Miami Beach: 305 538-3373
www.marriott.com
Experience this hotel's exciting guestroom makeover
featuring contemporary design with vibrant colors,
sophisticated artistic details and warm woods. Sitting on

two oceanfront acres, the hotel allows for breathtaking sunrise or moon-lit walks on the beach. Located less than two miles from South Beach's Art Deco District, the hotel offers both business-travel conveniences and boutique-style elegance with the comfort of resort amenities. Originally known as the Cadillac Hotel, the historic property reopened following a $40 million renovation to include spa services, private tiki beach, balconies on oceanfront guestrooms and much more.

CROYDON
3720 Collins Ave, Miami Beach, 305-938-1145
www.hotelcroydonmiamibeach.com
Designed in 1937 and formerly known as the Croydon Arms, this fully-renovated seven-story boutique hotel offers 104 guest rooms including a penthouse suite. Amenities include: flat-screen TVs, iPod docks, and complimentary Wi-Fi (in the lobby). Hotel features include: rooftop sundeck, outdoor pool, fitness center and spa. Nightclub and bowling alley on premises. Free airport shuttle and beach chairs.

EDEN ROC
4525 Collins Ave., Miami Beach: 305-520-7197

www.edenrochotelmiami.com
Just off a massive renovation. Iconic lobby bar must be seen. If you have to stay in Middle Beach, this is the place (or next door at the Fontainebleau).

FAENA
3201 Collins Ave, Miami Beach, 305-534-8800
www.faena.com/miami-beach
NEIGHBORHOOD: Mid-beach
Hot shot Argentine developer Alan Faena is responsible for this glamorous newly remodeled 1947 resort hotel (it's the old Saxony Hotel) that boasts beautifully designed art deco inspired rooms (58 rooms, 111 suites). He hired moviemaker Baz Luhrmann and his wife Catherine Martin and let them go all-out on this place, which has to be seen to be believed. Luhrmann, you might remember, remade "The Great Gatsby" with DiCaprio. And this hotel is as tarted up as Baz made Gatsby's Long Island mansion. The venue features a luxury spa, several high-end restaurants, including **Pao by Paul Qui** (a mix of Asian, Spanish and French influences) and **Los Fuegos by Francis Mallmann**, an Argentine grill master who cooks over open fires. (Get the rib eye with chimichurri—it'll be the best you've ever had). There's a big pool and a 150-seat cabaret-style theater. The lobby boasts 8 Juan Gatti murals. Outside in the garden is Damien Hirst's "Gone But Not Forgotten," a 24-karat gold & gilded skeleton of a giant woolly mammoth. Amenities include: complimentary Wi-Fi and on-site Fitness Center. Smoke-free hotel. This hotel is part of a six-block empire Faena has built up here in Middle Beach, and like I said, it's worth a short Uber / Lyft ride up here to have a good look at it all.

FONTAINEBLEAU
4441 Collins Ave., Miami Beach: 305 538-2000
www.fontainebleau.com/
One of two gloriously kitchy hotels (the other being next
door, the Eden Roc) designed by Morris Lapidus. This was
back in the mid '50s when Middle Beach became the
rising star and South Beach sank into the gutter of neglect.
After all, they didn't even have pools at the South Beach
hotels. Lapidus more than made up for it.

FREEHAND
(Formerly **Indian Creek Hotel**)
2727 Indian Creek Dr., Miami Beach: 305-531-2727
http://thefreehand.com/
Constructed in 1936, Indian Creek Hotel is my personal
favorite up in Middle Beach. It's as close to South Beach
as you can get without actually *being* there. Art Deco
masterpiece. Heated pool; 69 rooms. Now a happening
upmarket hostel.

LORRAINE HOTEL
2601 Collins Ave., Miami Beach: 305-538-7721
www.lorrainehotel.com

For the budget-minded traveler, here are airy and spacious rooms.

MIAMI BEACH EDITION
2901 Collins Ave, Miami Beach, 786-257-4500
www.editionhotels.com/miami-beach
Hotelier Ian Schrager and Marriott International have launched this luxury lifestyle hotel in the old Seville Hotel, renovated now into 294 guestrooms, including 28 bungalows and rooftop penthouses. Very posh, of course, like anything Schrager touches. Expect a lively bar scene and lots of activity in the Matador Room, Chef John-Georges Vongerichten's high-end on site eatery. Amenities include: complimentary Wi-Fi, iPod docks, and minibars. Hotel features include: Latin restaurant, outdoor lounge, nightclub, bowling alley, ice rink, spa, and a gym.

MIMOSA HOTEL
6525 Collins Ave., Miami Beach: 305-867-5000
www.themimosa.com
Oceanfront boutique hotel.

OCEAN SPRAY
4130 Collins Ave., Miami Beach: 305-535-5300
www.oceanspraymiami.com
Totally renovated — retaining its classic 1934 Art Deco exterior and lobby design — with chic, European guest and meeting room furnishings.

SOHO BEACH HOUSE
4385 Collins Ave., Miami Beach: 786-507-7900
www.sohobeachhouse.com
Swankest place up in this neighborhood. This private members club, hotel and spa are located on the site of the Sovereign Hotel. The site has been entirely redesigned and expanded to include a 16-story oceanfront tower.

Overlooking the ocean, it includes 50 bedrooms, a private beach, and an expansive Cowshed spa and gym. There are two pools, indoor and outdoor dining, secluded gardens, a screening room and **Cecconi's restaurant** open to the public.

WESTGATE
3611 Collins Ave., Miami Beach: 305-532-8831
www.wgsouthbeach.com
This newly renovated beachfront resort is the perfect marriage of quaint intimacy and contemporary comfort.

DOWNTOWN / BRICKELL

A lot of fancy hotels have populated Miami's Downtown/Brickell Corridor in recent years, helping by their presence to elevate what for *decades* has been one of the more wretched downtown areas of any major U.S. city. And most of Downtown is still pretty much of an eyesore. But while Downtown still has its undeniably seedy side, none of this is apparent in its selection of hotels.

CONRAD MIAMI
1395 Brickell Ave., Miami - 305 503-6500
http://conradhotels3.hilton.com/en/hotels/florida/conrad-miami-MIACICI/index.html
Great location on the Bay, this is Hilton's "upscale" brand. Beautiful surroundings for people doing business with a flare (well, on an expense account). Has a notable spa. The 25th floor is home to a fancy restaurant.

COURTYARD BY MARRIOTT
200 SE 2nd Ave., Miami - 305 374-3000
www.marriott.com/hotels/travel/miadt-courtyard-miami-downtown-brickell-area

Has 231 rooms with balconies (27 of which are one-bedroom suites). Near Bayside Marketplace, Brickell Avenue Financial District and the Port of Miami. Free high-speed Internet access in guest rooms, and free wireless access in public areas. The hotel works with several companies to provide transportation to the Port of Miami for a fee of $5 per person.

DOUBLETREE BY HILTON GRAND

1717 N. Bayshore Drive, Miami - 305 372-0313
www.doubletree3.hilton.com/en/hotels/florida/doubletree-by-hilton-grand-hotel-biscayne-bay-MIABSDT/index.html
Hotel and condo complex up in what is still called Omni Area, 10 blocks north of Downtown. Great views of Biscayne Bay. Offers a full range of amenities. Close to the Port of Miami, shopping, the Downtown Miami Business District.

EPIC HOTEL

270 Biscayne Blvd. Way, Miami - 305 424-5226
www.epichotel.com
This top spot is on the Miami River where it meets the Bay. Part of Kimpton Hotels, this boutique hotel epitomizes urban design while offering guests an unmatched level of style and service. This hotel operates on a grand scale with an authenticity that attracts travelers from around the globe.

EUROSTARS LANGFORD

121 SE 1st St, Miami, 305-250-0782
www.eurostarshotels.com
NEIGHBORHOOD: Downtown
Formerly the Miami National Bank, this iconic building has been reimagined as a 126-room luxury hotel. This architectural gem has been lovingly preserved and offers high-tech amenities. Rooms come equipped with 48" HD

flat-screen TVs, complimentary Wi-Fi, and MP3/iPod docking stations. Hotel features include: on-site restaurant, rooftop bar and lounge, and exercise studio.

FOUR SEASONS
1435 Brickell Ave., Miami - 305 358-3535
www.fourseasons.com/miami
Sleek tower of luxurious guest rooms and suites offers sweeping vistas and resort-style amenities.

HILTON MIAMI
1601 Biscayne Blvd., Miami - 305 374-0000
www.hiltonmiamidowntown.com
A Metromover connection provides convenient access around the city. Shuttle service to the Port of Miami through a company located in the hotel lobby, for a fee with advance reservations. Just minutes from Bayside Marketplace, the Design District and Midtown Miami.

HILTON GARDEN INN MIAMI BRICKELL SOUTH
2500 Brickell Ave., Miami - 305-854-2070
www.hilton.com
This hotel offers the ultimate boutique accommodations at moderate prices for both business and leisure. Featuring three floors with 65 stylish guest rooms, which have walk-in showers, balconies or lanais, lovely interiors and free high-speed Internet.

HOLIDAY INN PORT OF MIAMI
340 Biscayne Blvd., Miami - 305 371-4400
https://www.ihg.com
Directly across the street from Bayside Marketplace and opposite the Port of Miami. It is within easy walking distance to the Miami Convention Center, American Airlines Arena, the financial district and Government

Center. A MetroMover stop is located behind the parking lot. (This is more important than you think.)

HOTEL BEAUX ARTS MIAMI
255 Biscayne Blvd. Way, 39th Floor, Miami - 305 421-8700
www.hotelbeauxartsmiami.com
This boutique property is so exclusive, most people have never heard of it. About as good as it gets in Downtown. Situated on the 39th floor, this hotel is an architectural masterpiece offering the most discriminating and sophisticated business and leisure traveler dramatic city and bay views with total exclusivity. Entirely outfitted with Bang & Olufsen in-room entertainment systems, the hotel is a private urban retreat providing guests with services such as private check-in and personal escort to one of the 44 ultra-contemporary and lavishly appointed guest rooms and suites.

HYATT REGENCY MIAMI
400 SE 2nd Ave., Miami - 305 358-1234
https://miami.regency.hyatt.com/en/hotel/home.html
On the scenic Riverwalk attached to the Miami Convention Center. Recently completed a $20 million renovation. Featuring the new Hyatt StayFit TM Fitness Center and newly updated heated outdoor pool. Direct access to MetroMover for transportation around Downtown and to shopping and area attractions. Conveniently located to the Port of Miami, Bayside Marketplace and American Airlines Arena.

INTERCONTINENTAL MIAMI
100 Chopin Plaza, Miami - 305 577-1000
www.icmiamihotel.com
Located on Biscayne Bay, adjacent to Bayside Marketplace and Bayfront Park. Elegantly appointed hotel

offers luxurious guest rooms and a full range of first-class facilities.

JW MARRIOTT MARQUIS
255 Biscayne Blvd. Way, Miami - 305 421-8600
www.marriott.com
The high-end in the Marriott brand, this is centrally located Downtown, and is notable because **Daniel Boulud** has his restaurant here.

JW MARRIOTT HOTEL MIAMI
1109 Brickell Ave., Miami - 305 329-3500
www.marriott.com/miajw
The "other" Marriott Downtown. It blends the features of a premier conference and meeting facility with excellent service. Elegantly furnished guest rooms and suites offer the finest details, including marble tubs, high-speed Internet and flat-screen televisions. Delicious dining options range from the wine-inspired contemporary cuisine of **Isabela's** to the casual fare at **La Terraza Cafe and Bar.** Relaxation is as close as the luxurious spa and the unique stainless pool.

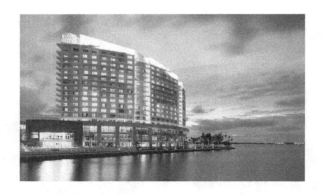

MANDARIN ORIENTAL
500 Brickell Key Drive, Miami - 305 913-8288
www.mandarinoriental.com/miami
A waterfront urban resort located on prestigious Brickell
Key, featuring spacious guest rooms and suites, state-of-
the-art conference and banquet facilities, a five-star
holistic **Spa** and fitness center, and a world-class on-site
Beach Club. The hotel is also affiliated with Brickell
Tennis Club and Crandon Golf Course. Lots of celebs stay
here, or more often dine here.

RODEWAY INN & SUITES
100 SE 4th St., Miami, 305-374-5100
https://www.choicehotels.com/
Ideally situated in the heart of Downtown Miami on the
Miami River, this upscale property offers suites and hotel
rooms, with a full-service restaurant, lounge, business
center, wireless Internet in all rooms, gym, pool and valet
parking.

W MIAMI
485 Brickell Ave., Miami - 305 503-4400
www.wmiamihotel.com
This boutique hotel is always in the news because so many
famous people stay here. Designed by Kelly Wearstler, it

juxtaposes elite residential necessities with scene-making dining, roof-raising lounging. Set within the 10-acre Icon Brickell enclave, this urban resort is replete with skyscraping residential towers, two parks, a 28,000-square-foot spa and fitness center, and a two-acre outdoor living room bedecked by a 300-foot long pool, oversized outdoor fireplace, and more lifestyle flights of fancy.

COCONUT GROVE

The Grove was THE place to be before South Beach came roaring along in the mid to late '80s to dominate nightlife and entertainment. The club at the Mutiny (what was the owner's name, Barton Goldberg, right?) was the center of activity, and all nightlife in Miami emanated from the Grove.

After the Mariel Boatlift in '80 deposited thousands of poor Cubans (and a lot of criminals as Castro bragged about emptying his jails on a doofus President Carter), the Grove became even hotter because all the Cuban refugees lived in South Beach, then the poorest part of town (and a good time to buy for those smart enough to see ahead).

Anyway, today the Grove has a lot of empty storefronts for rent, the restaurants are so-so and the nightlife: nothing to speak of.

Still, many see and appreciate the Grove's unique charm. Its residential areas are among the nicest in town. And the Grove will always have its champions. (Having been born there, I am one of them.)

Its hotels, in the meantime, continue to boast some big names and quality environments for the discriminating traveler.

In fact, the Grove is a *great* place to go if you want *out* of frenetic South Beach. And they'd be wise to begin an advertising campaign along the lines of the "Come to Miami and experience the *UN*-South Beach."

COURTYARD BY MARRIOTT
2649 S. Bayshore Drive, Miami - 305 858-2500
www.courtyardmiamicoconutgrove.com
20-floor high-rise building features breathtaking views of Miami and Biscayne Bay. It includes 196 spacious guest rooms, including 20 suites. Complimentary Wi-Fi throughout the hotel. Most guest rooms have balconies.

HOTEL ARYA COCONUT GROVE
2889 McFarlane Rd., Coconut Grove - 305-529-2828
www.hotelaryacg.com
Nice place with all the usual amenities. The restaurant on the 8th floor, **Panorama** offers a wide variety of traditional American and Nuevo-Andean Peruvian cuisine.

MAYFAIR HOTEL & SPA
3000 Florida Ave., Coconut Grove - 305 441-0000
www.mayfairhotelandspa.com
This landmark hotel has a new Cabana Rooftop Pool & Lounge with cabanas, an infinity chic pool and spectacular views of Biscayne Bay and Miami's skyline.

MUTINY HOTEL
2951 S. Bayshore Drive, Coconut Grove - 305 441-2100
http://www.mutinyhotel.com
The scene of many wild nights in the '70s and '80s before South Beach came along to steal away the Grove's thunder. The most decadent place in the Cocaine Cowboy Days. The restaurant (private club) was quite unique, had 3 levels and a famous metal membership card with a pirate face on it. (Don't get me started on those "themed" rooms where everybody partied.)

This place fell into disrepair and has been completely refurbished into a modern property.

Its one- and two-bedroom apartment suites are decorated in a "British Colonial" style featuring rich hardwood furnishings, fine Bay views. Every modern convenience and amenity is available, with separate living/dining areas, including a Queen sleeper sofa in the living room, a fully equipped kitchen and European-style bathrooms; flat screen televisions and more. Many suites offer private balconies with city and water views; many units also offer washer/dryer, complimentary upon request. In-room amenities include: Hair dryer, lighted make-up mirror, Fully Equipped Kitchen, flat screen TVs, iPod clock Radios.

RESIDENCE INN BY MARRIOTT
2835 Tigertail Ave., Coconut Grove - 305 285-9303
http://www.residenceinn.com/miaco
An all-suite hotel within walking distance from CocoWalk and the shops, dining and nightlife of the Grove. Free daily buffet breakfast, high-speed Internet access, and evening socials on select days.

RITZ-CARLTON
3300 SW 27th Ave., Coconut Grove - 305 644-4680
www.ritzcarlton.com
Yes, there's even a Ritz-Carlton in the Grove to go with the ones in Key Biscayne and South Beach. This one has a charming, villa-like ambience, soaring ceilings, Venetian stucco columns, fragrant roses, a grand fireplace (you won't need THAT in summer!) and picturesque views.

KEY BISCAYNE

RITZ-CARLTON
455 Grand Bay Dr., Key Biscayne: 305-365-4500
www.ritzcarlton.com
Oceanfront resort with a superior "tropical" ambience.
About as far from the South Beach "thing" as you can
possibly get without going to Maine. Best thing about this
place is the huge (over 20,000 square feet) spa. Excellent
tennis facilities and, well—they have just about anything
you can imagine (except excitement, unless you're
sleeping with one of the staff). Great place to come to
recuperate from a facelift.

CORAL GABLES

THE BILTMORE
1200 Anastasia Ave, Coral Gables, 855 311-6903
http://www.biltmorehotel.com
This National Historic Landmark is located in the
exclusive Coral Gables area. The 273-room hotel reflects

classic Italian, Moorish, and Spanish architectural influences spread over 150 acres of tropical landscaping. A favorite of world leaders and notables since its opening in 1926, the hotel offers a restored Donald Ross 18-hole, 71 par championship golf course, tennis, one of the largest hotel pools in the country, private cabanas, a European spa, and an award-winning fitness center. The hotel's dining destinations include the acclaimed **Palme d'Or**, which Zagat calls one of the best restaurants in the country; and Fontana, an Italian restaurant surrounding the Biltmore fountain.

COURTYARD BY MARRIOTT
2051 Le Jeune Road, Coral Gables: 305 443-2301
www.marriott.com
This hotel is located three blocks from the Coral Gables business district and two miles south of MIA, within walking distance of great shopping, dining and area attractions. It features renovated guest rooms and complimentary airport transportation.

HOTEL ST. MICHEL
162 Alcazar Ave., Coral Gables: 305-444-1666
www.hotelstmichel.com
This is a tiny gem (only 28 rooms) right in the heart of things. Feels *totally* unlike anything in Miami, and is where I prefer to stay when I am forced to be in the Gables. Feels like a country inn. It's in a building that went up in 1926 as the Sevilla Hotel. They have a tour desk, free WiFi, flat-screen TVs, free continental breakfast.

HYATT REGENCY
50 Alhambra Plaza, Coral Gables: 305 441-1234
https://coralgables.regency.hyatt.com

An elegant Mediterranean-style hotel inspired by Spain's Alhambra Palace. Newly renovated guest rooms are appointed with luxurious furnishings and offer spacious living areas. Located in the center of Coral Gables and close to dining, shopping and entertainment. Wireless high-speed Internet access is available.

HOTEL COLONNADE

180 Aragon Ave., Coral Gables: 305 441-2600
www.hotelcolonnade.com/
Centrally located in the business and retail district of Coral Gables. Recognized by Conde Nast Traveler as one of the top 500 hotels in the world. The hotel has ample meeting space to accommodate groups from 10 to 700 people. The Regus Business Center allows business travelers the opportunity to rent a furnished office in the hotel, with convenient features such as high-speed Internet access.

CHAPTER 3
RESTAURANTS

INTRODUCTION
Miami-Dade Food Tours
SOUTH BEACH
(Ridiculously Extravagant - Sensible Alternatives - Quality Bargain Spots)
MIDDLE & NORTH BEACHES
(Bal Harbour, Surfside) **MIAMI NORTH**
DESIGN DISTRICT-MIDTOWN-BISCAYNE
CORRIDOR
DOWNTOWN-BRICKELL
LITTLE HAVAVA
CORAL GABLES
COCONUT GROVE
KEY BISCAYNE

INTRODUCTION

The greatest pleasure for me has been to witness firsthand the explosion of culinary diversity that has made Greater Miami one of the most interesting "food towns" in the U.S.

Not to take anything away from New Orleans or Charleston or Savannah or any other locale in America that boasts a distinctive cuisine, but I can safely say Miami's offerings are terribly more interesting and culturally engaging than any town in the U.S. besides New York.

Why?

Because the cuisines in New Orleans and places like Baltimore—while among the best America has to offer—are generally quite static. Sorry, folks, but in the end, shrimp and grits are still shrimp and grits. That soft-shelled crab at that little shack on the Chesapeake—it's the same year in and year out.

But when was the last time you went to a restaurant and had Guatemalan food? Or Peruvian.

All right—I admit the cuisines you can expect to find in Miami will have a Latin slant—but what's wrong with that? You'll find such a huge variety of cuisines you've never tried before. You'll travel a long, long way from the black beans and rice of a Cuban meal to a ceviche made by a Peruvian.

The excitement generated by the nightlife industry, climate and cultural diversity one gets in Miami has attracted a Who's Who of famous international chefs. The unqualified success of the **Food Network South Beach Wine & Food Festival** (directly attributable to the obsessive single-mindedness of **Lee Brian Schrager** of **Southern Wine & Spirits**) brought chefs from all over the world to South Beach. Many who came, saw what they liked, and opened outposts in their global empires here on the sandy shores of the Billion Dollar Sandbar.

But a big name in France or New York is no guarantee of success. **David Bouley's** aptly named "Evolution" in the Ritz-Carlton might have easily been named "Natural Selection" because it closed within a year. South Beach is as tough a town as New York or anywhere else where the public is fickle and the rents are as sky high as a chef's ambition.

But the good news is that there seems to be a new opening every week.

MIAMI-DADE FOOD TOURS

If you don't want to do your homework, consider following a guide as you tour the area. I've done a couple of these and they're really quite fun.

MIAMI CULINARY TOURS
LOCATIONS: Little Havana, South Beach, Miami City
Tours: 786-942-8856
www.miamiculinarytours.com
COST: Rates vary by season (special rates for children, military)

FOOD TOURS OF MIAMI
LOCATIONS: Coral Gables and South Beach
www.foodtoursofmiami.com and
www.pubcrawlofmiami.com
COST: Rates vary by season (special rates for children, military)

SOUTH BEACH
Ridiculously Extravagant
Sensible Alternatives
Quality Bargain Spots

APPLE A DAY
1534 Alton Rd, 305-538-4569
www.appleadaymiami.com
WEBSITE DOWN AT PRESSTIME
CUISINE: Juice bar/Smoothies

DRINKS: No Booze
SERVING: 8 a.m. – 10 p.m.
PRICE RANGE: $$
Health food market offering usual health food items plus
fresh juices, salads, and wraps. Favorites: Vegan pizza and
variety of tacos. Raw vitamins and supplements. Counter-
service with seating indoors & out.

AURA AT BOOKS & BOOKS
927 Lincoln Rd.; 305-695-8898
No web site
CUISINE: Contemporary, Eclectic; some good Cuban
DRINKS: Beer & Wine
SERVING: Breakfast, lunch and dinner daily
Take a minute to look up at the historic Sterling Building
in which this café is housed. It's one of the best examples
of "Streamline Moderne" Art Deco architecture in the
country. I used to have an office in this building and loved
walking to work there every day. Excellent spot for
breakfast, lunch or dinner on Lincoln Road, which you
may consider a big fat Tourist Trap with a bunch of
overpriced eateries with boring food served indifferently.
That's not true in this place.

AZABU
Marriott Stanton South Beach
161 Ocean Dr, Miami Beach, 786-276-0520
https://azabuglobal.com
CUISINE: Sushi/Japanese
DRINKS: Full bar
SERVING: Dinner only
PRICE RANGE: $$$$
NEIGHBORHOOD: SoFi (South of Fifth)
Tucked away off the lobby of this waterfront Marriott is an
upscale eatery with a fixed price menu featuring an open
kitchen and bar are. The light stained wood paneling looks

striking because it is mounted horizontally, and matches the light color of the wooden bar where you sit in the Den and look on while the chefs work creating your meal. Clean, pristine, Spartan surroundings. Very efficient service (not something we're terribly used to on casual South Beach). The lighting is very cleverly designed, with pin spots in one place and recessed lighting elsewhere, all very romantic. The Robata Bar is completely different, with the countertop where you sit dominated by a busy swirling marble design. There's a beautiful shellfish display when you walk in—all the raw food that will soon be your dinner. Expect to sit for 2 hours. Great sushi offerings including Japanese barracuda, Tuna kama, and Tempura Whole Squid. The place is not cheap, so if you're on a budget, take advantage of their Happy Hour 6-8 p.m.

BAOLI
1908 Collins Ave., Miami Beach, 305-674-8822
www.baoli-group.com
CUISINE: French, Italian
DRINKS: Full Bar
SERVING: Dinner
PRICE RANGE: $$$$
As good as the food is, the best thing about Baoli is the charming patio-courtyard with a canopy of shade trees sprinkled with lights that give the place an other-worldly feel. A big menu covers all the bases, from a raw bar to sushi to a great selection of pastas (black truffle risotto) to grilled items (an 18oz grilled rib eye), to seafood (get the bouillabaisse). Oh, that "other-worldly" feel? You'll come back to this world when they bring you the check.

BARTON G: THE RESTAURANT
1427 West Ave.; 305-672-8881
www.bartongtherestaurant.com
CUISINE: American, Contemporary

DRINKS: Full bar
SERVING: Dinner nightly from 6
PRICE RANGE: $$$$
The expensive (and expensively famous) creation of
Barton G. An experience you won't forget. When you
come here, throw caution to the wind and surrender
yourself. Worth every penny. (I went there on my birthday
and ordered a three-pound lobster tail: we were eating
lobster salad for two days!)

BAYSIDE GRILL
The Standard Hotel; 40 Island Ave.; 786-245-0880;
CUISINE: Greek, Mediterranean, International; DRINKS:
Full bar; SERVING: Daily 7am-midnight; WEB:
www.standardhotels.com
PRICE RANGE: $$$
There are damn few places where you can have a drink
and see Biscayne Bay. (Even on Ocean Drive, the park is
between you and the water and you can't see the ocean,
either, except way out.) Well, over here on the first island
on the Venetian Causeway, you'll find a perfect spot. It's
got a pool, a restaurant, a spa. L.A. hotelier Andre Balazs
bought the rundown Lido Spa and renovated it into one of
his hip Standard hotels. It's just stunning at sunset by the
pool. (The French fries are the best!) Note: there's
nowhere to park, so you *have* to valet if you drive. Take an
Uber. $$$

BARCELONETA
1400 20th St, Miami Beach, 305-538-9299
http://barcelonetamiami.com
CUISINE: Spanish
DRINKS: Full bar
SERVING: Lunch/Dinner
PRICE RANGE: $$
NEIGHBORHOOD: Sunset Harbour

Popular storefront eatery with a menu of small plates of typical Spanish fare. The name comes from "La Barceloneta," which is the section of Barcelona built in the 18th Century and is home to the big broad beach area of the town. People come here to go to the beach, have fun, eat tapas, you name it. Whenever I'm in Barcelona (which is never too often, as I love the place), I stay in the L'Eixample area, but I never fail to come down to La Barceloneta for some great seafood you find in little spots off the beaten tourist trap. Here on South Beach, it's a little different, but their heart's in the right place. Plenty of outdoor tables as well as a spacious indoor area. A small cozy bar in the corner where you'll find me sitting, drinking and eating when I stop in. Favorites include: Steak tartar and Spicy shrimp. Great wine selection. Great casual dining environment. (The marina is just across the street, so you'll find people from the boats docked there dropping in here all the time—they come from all over the world, so you never know who you'll meet.) The food's not *quite* as good as it is in La Barceloneta, but, hey, it comes close and, more important, makes me sigh happily every time I take a bite.

THE BAZAAR BY JOSÉ ANDRÉS
SLS HOTEL
1701 Collins Ave., Miami Beach: 305-455-2999
www.thebazaar.com
CUISINE: Tapas/Small Plates, Spanish
DRINKS: Full Bar
SERVING: Dinner
The swanky SLS Hotel had to have a big name to headline its "important" restaurant, and it's hard to top **José Andrés**. Fun place with a creative menu serving items like Dragonfruit Ceviche and Caprese Salad. Delicious cocktails. Great selection of Serrano and Ibérico hams, Catalan pork sausage, codfish fritters (a specialty), seared

scallops. Though I never liked it, everybody raves about the Dulce de Leche dessert. $$$$

BIG PINK
157 Collins Ave.; 305-532-4700; 305-531-0888 for delivery.
http://www.mylesrestaurantgroup.com/
CUISINE: American, Diner
DRINKS: Full bar
SERVING: Breakfast, lunch and dinner from 8am.
NEIGHBORHOOD: SoFi (South of Fifth)
TVs for sports fans. You'd never know it to walk in this joint, but the same guy who owns **Prime 112** a couple of blocks away owns this place slinging out chicken wings and draft beer for pennies on the dollar compared to the higher-profile place. Really good American diner food. Popular with locals who wouldn't be caught dead at Prime 112. $$

BODEGA TAQUERIA Y TEQUILA
1220 16th St, Miami Beach, 305-704-2145
www.bodegasouthbeach.com
CUISINE: Mexican
DRINKS: Full Bar
SERVING: Lunch & Dinner
PRICE RANGE: $$
This local's favorite serves over-the-top Mexican street food and features a taco truck inside. Great choice for lunch or late-night munching. The real star of this place is the hidden bar.

BOLIVAR
841 Washington Ave., Miami Beach: 305-305-0801
www.bolivarmiamibeach.com
CUISINE: Peruvian, Colombian, Venezuelan
DRINKS: Full Bar

SERVING: Lunch, Dinner
Classic South American dishes served. Delicious menu items include salmon in Creole sauce with cilantro rice. Romantic atmosphere and excellent service. $$

BYBLOS
1545 Collins Ave, Miami Beach, 786-864-2990
www.byblosmiami.com
CUISINE: Mediterranean / Middle Eastern
DRINKS: Full bar
SERVING: Dinner
PRICE RANGE: $$$
This place offers a great dining experience in a plush atmosphere that makes you imagine what Nikki Beach might look like in Greece. (Or anywhere else out there.) High ceilings, lush booths, pillows, divans, lounges. The cuisine is a mishmash of items from Jordan, Israel, Lebanon. All very tasty and very expertly prepared. This place opened after the Canadian owners had a big success with a Byblos in Toronto. Unlike a lot of other upmarket restaurants flooding into Miami, this one is not pretentious and full of itself. Even if you don't like Lamb Ribs, I urge you to get it as a starter. They marinate them 24 hours before they get a rubbing of molasses. Then the ribs are plunked into a blend of Eastern spices & crushed nuts and seeds (called dukka) that results in a crunchy texture to the finished product. Anyway, they are really good. There are numerous delicious dishes like Duck Kibbeh, Eggplant Dumplings and Jeweled Rice. If you know someone who knows this kind of food, treat them to dinner here—they'll help you order. Otherwise, trust the very friendly staff. The wine list is more expensive than it ought to be, so order wisely. Or drink beer, as I do, even better.

CARROT EXPRESS
1755 Alton Rd, 305-535-1379

www.carrotexpressmiamibeachfl.com
CUISINE: Vegetarian/Juice Bar
DRINKS: No Booze
SERVING: 10 a.m. – 9 p.m.
PRICE RANGE: $$
Counter-service spot offering a menu of vegan &
vegetarian fare. Favorites: Chicken melt on pita and Tuna
wrap. Great smoothies.

CASA TUA
1700 James Ave.; 305-673-1010
www.casatualifestyle.com/miami/
CUISINE: Italian, with a flair
DRINKS: Full bar
SERVING: Lunch weekdays 12pm – 3pm; dinner nightly
from 7
Very hot spot. The best food. Upstairs they have a VERY
nice lounge, but it's private now. (I used to love the
upstairs lounge for a drink or two before dining below.)
But plebeians can still get in for lunch and dinner. But the
food doesn't get much better. A lovely starter is the veal
tartare with artichokes and truffles. They have a veal
tenderloin marinated in lime served with an au gratin of
zucchini that melts in your mouth; also braised veal cheeks
that are sublime. They have two risottos that are standouts:
the one with the Maine lobster and the one with black
truffles. Superior. The lunch menu is very abbreviated.
Here, splurge on dinner, even if you might get treated like
the ultimate Outsider.

CHALAN ON THE BEACH
1580 Washington Ave.; 305-532-8880
No web site
CUISINE: Peruvian
DRINKS: Beer & wine
SERVING: Lunch and dinner daily

It looks like a trashy dump on the outside, but once you slide indoors, you can expect some of the best Peruvian food to be had in Miami. And cheap, too. No other Latin America culture prepares seafood as well as Peruvians, in my view. If you're not familiar with this cuisine, the menu will dazzle you. $$

CHEESEBURGER BABY
1505 Washington Ave.; 305-531-7300
CUISINE: the great American burger
DRINKS: beer & wine
SERVING: lunch and dinner daily. Delivery day and night
www.cheeseburgerbaby.net
There's been a proliferation of burger joints on South Beach in the last couple of years, but these are without question the **JUICIEST BURGERS** in South Beach. You can't beat this joint anywhere. All beef is certified Angus, the buns baked locally and the hand-cut their own toppings. The place has a great dive atmosphere. The food, however, is anything but. Counter seating. Only female-owned burger joint and food truck in Miami, since 2001. You go, girls!

CHOTTO MATTE
1664 Lenox Ave, Miami Beach, 305-690-0743
https://chotto-matte.com/miami/
CUISINE: Japanese/Peruvian
DRINKS: Full bar
SERVING: Lunch & Dinner
PRICE RANGE: $$$$
NEIGHBORHOOD: Lincoln Road
Upscale hidden gem located off iconic Lincoln Road with a menu of Nikkei (Japanese & Peruvian) cuisine served "tapas" size. (It's an offshoot of a hip trendy place in London.) There's a dramatic cluster of palm trees raised in the center island behind the bar, and this stands below a

very tall atrium that gives the room a majestic ambience. As good as the food is, my advice would be to avoid the weekends, when they start the DJ music as early as 8, making conversation completely impossible. Service drags on. I was once there for over 3 hours and hated every minute of it. Better to come any night but Friday or Saturday. Beautiful décor. Spacious bar with a lively scene. Better yet, do it for lunch unless you want the excitement generated by a crowded place. Favorites: Lobster tempura and Wagyu dumplings. Hang out at the bar for one of their creative cocktails. (I know because I went to the bar more than once to get a drink when the waiter kept avoiding our table.)

CLEO SOUTH BEACH
1776 Collins Ave, Miami Beach, 305-534-2536
www.sbe.com/cleosouthbeach
CUISINE: Mediterranean/Middle Eastern
DRINKS: Full Bar
SERVING: Dinner
PRICE RANGE: $$$
Located in the hip Redbury Hotel, this modern eatery offers a nice menu of creative Eastern Mediterranean fare. The owners came in from L.A. to launch this place and they brought an extremely competent staff to get things rolling. A very welcoming atmosphere. Menu picks include: Grilled octopus and Tuna Tartare. Nice large bar, which is where you'll find me chatting with the bartender, who makes a powerfully effective Manhattan with Makers Mark.

DECK SIXTEEN
1600 Collins Ave, Miami Beach, 305-695-7400
https://southbeachmiami.centric.hyatt.com
CUISINE: Spanish / Mediterranean

DRINKS: Full bar
SERVING: Dinner nightly
PRICE RANGE: $$
Located on third floor of Hyatt Centric hotel, offering a
menu of Spanish-Mediterranean fare. Chef William
Milian's creative menu includes favorites like: Octopus
with Giant Beans and Chorizo with little potatoes.
Indoor/outdoor seating.

DORAKU
1104 Lincoln Rd.; 305-695-8383
CUISINE: Japanese/Sushi.
DRINKS: Full bar; SERVING: lunch and dinner daily;
www.dorakusushi.com.
Among the dozen places on Lincoln Road where you can
get sushi (and I've eaten in all of them multiple times
because that's my job), this is the one I always come back
to when I'm not forced by work to go elsewhere. (Has one
of the few lively bar scenes among Lincoln Road
restaurants and a nice if unpublicized Happy Hour good
for food as well as drinks.) $$$

DRUNKEN DRAGON
1424 Alton Rd, Miami Beach, 305-397-8556
www.drunkendragon.com
CUISINE: Asian Fusion / Korean
DRINKS: Full Bar
SERVING: Dinner
PRICE RANGE: $$
This exceedingly popular Korean eatery featuring Asian
Fusion and BBQ took over an old Cuban market and never
bothered changing the nondescript big red sign out front
that reads, simply enough, MARKET. And for some
reason, it's wildly popular, so much so you'll need to book
ahead. South Beach's first Korean barbecue restaurant
offers tableside grilling and modern Asian tapas.

ESTIATORIO MILOS BY COSTAS SPILIADIS
730 First St., Miami Beach: 305-604-6800
www.estiatoriomilos.com
CUISINE: Greek, Seafood
DRINKS: Full Bar
SERVING: Lunch, Dinner
The name alone tells you how "important" they are. When did restaurants become movies, with the director's name above the title? "A Steven Spielberg Eatery." But they do deliver the goods here: incredible choice of seafood shipped in from Morocco, Tunisia, Portugal, Nova Scotia and Greece. Though they have a great selection of meats, you'll want to focus on the seafood here. If you want to savor their excellent food but don't want to pay the bill (this is one of the most expensive places in town), stop in for lunch when they have a prix fixe menu for less than $30. I come here for lunch at least once a month, dinner once a year. Excellent wine list, almost all Greek selections that are light and refreshing. $$$$

FOGO DE CHAO
836 First St.; 305-672-0011
www.fogodechao.com.
CUISINE: Brazilian Steakhouse
DRINKS: Full bar
SERVING: lunch weekdays; dinner nightly
NEIGHBORHOOD: SoFi (South of Fifth)
Great experience. Massive salad bar comes with your meal
(which is *prix fixe*, and it's all you can eat). Waiters
carrying swords with grilled meat move table-to-table
supplying you with an endless amount of different kinds of
meat. If you're from the middle of nowhere, this is a must.
They won't have this in your town. (I'm just glad they
have it in this town!) Excellent and reasonable wine list
and the most attentive staff. (It's a little heavy for lunch, so
if you come for lunch, make this your big meal of the day.)
$$

FORTE DEI MARMI
150 Ocean Dr, Miami Beach,786-276-3095

www.fdmmiami.com
CUISINE: Italian/Seafood
DRINKS: Full Bar
SERVING: Dinner, Sunday Brunch
PRICE RANGE: $$$
Chic eatery offering a creative menu of Italian classics in a
lovely setting. Pink bougainvillea hangs from the arched
entrance. Favorites: Linguine Alla Nerano and Calamari
Tagliatelle. Great place for Sunday Brunch. If you're
having dessert you must try the Sicilian's Pistachio Crème
Brulee, an interesting version of crème brulee served with
chocolate gelato. All-Italian wine list.

JAYA AT SETAI
2001 Collins Ave., 855-923-7899
CUISINE: Contemporary, Indian
DRINKS: Full bar
SERVING: 7am to midnight daily
www.thesetaihotel.com
Just plain excellent. Fine food beautifully served. In a
town with several really good Sunday brunches, this one
excels. It's not the cheapest, but it may very well be the
best.

JOE'S STONE CRAB $$$
11 Washington Ave.; 305-673-0365
www.joesstonecrab.com
CUISINE: American, Seafood
DRINKS: Full bar
SERVING: lunch, dinner daily October-May; summer
hours vary
NEIGHBORHOOD: SoFi (South of Fifth)
The most famous restaurant on South Beach. Opened in
1913, they still serve up great stone crabs. If you don't like
stone crabs (I actually met someone who didn't!), order
anything on their menu. It's all great. You can even get
half a fried chicken for $6.95, some of the best fried
chicken you've ever had. If you've never been here before,
this is a must. But it's much easier at lunch than dinner to
get in. If you have to go to dinner, go early, around 6, and
getting in won't be a problem. Later than that, expect a
wait of an hour or two, longer on weekends. (A great place
to eat at the bar if you're alone or a couple.) No
reservations.

JOE'S TAKEAWAY

11 Washington Ave., 305-673-4611
CUISINE: American
DRINKS: Beer & Wine
SERVING: breakfast, lunch, dinner daily; closed in
summer
www.joesstonecrab.com
NEIGHBORHOOD: SoFi (South of Fifth)
They even serve breakfast (I have breakfast here 3 times a
week when I am in town), and things here are cheaper than
you think. There are dozens of restaurants on South Beach
that charge more than Joe's for inferior quality food and
service. (Try their fried chicken—you get a half-chicken
for an astounding $6.95.) $$

JUVIA

1111 Lincoln Rd., Miami Beach: 305-763-8272
www.juviamiami.com
CUISINE: Asian Fusion, Japanese, Seafood
DRINKS: Full Bar
SERVING: Lunch, Dinner
Gorgeous setting with penthouse views of South Beach.
Creative menu with dishes like Unagi with chocolate and
Binchotan-grilled tenderloin. Dine early for sunset view.
There are surprisingly few places where you can get an
overview of South Beach. This is one of them. If you're on
a budget, go to the bar, enjoy the view and eat somewhere
else. **Shake Shack's** in the same building.) Order a beer,
which will cost less than a glass of wine and last longer.
$$$$

KATSUYA BY STARCK
SLS Hotel

1701 Collins Ave., Miami Beach: 305-455-2995
www.sbe.com/katsuya/south-beach
CUISINE: Sushi

DRINKS: Full Bar
SERVING: Dinner
A chic two-level sushi restaurant in South Beach's new **SLS Hotel** with a menu of small starters, sushi, robata and other hot dishes. Extensive list of sake and specialty cocktails. $$$$

LA SANDWICHERIE
229 14 St., Miami Beach: 305-532-8934
www.lasandwicherie.com
CUISINE: Sandwiches; French
DRINKS: beer & wine
SERVING: 8 a.m. to 5 a.m. (till 6 a.m. on weekends)
Whoever figured this place would last for 20 years? I first came across this placed stumbling out of South Beach's oldest (and still the best) dive bar across the street, the **Deuce**. It's just a little spot, with an outdoor counter and no indoor seating. Nice sandwiches ($6-$9) always served on crunchy baguettes of soft croissants. You can sort of make each sandwich to order. It's like the archetypal Subway, only they wish.

LT STEAK & SEAFOOD
The Betsy Hotel
1440 Ocean Dr., 305-673-0044
www.thebetsyhotel.com/dining
CUISINE: Steaks-some seafood

DRINKS: Full bar
SERVING: Breakfast, lunch and dinner daily
Chef Laurent Tourondel's entry in the South Beach
restaurant sweepstakes. Not just the steaks for which he's
famous, but Dover sole and other seafood specialties as
well. Breakfast for two can run you a cool $60. A recent
dinner for four cost over $500. So... make it a special
occasion, because it IS special. Extremely talented and
attentive waiters. (The best bacon in the world if you have
a chance to breakfast here. Worth a special trip for the
bacon and scones in the morning.) This is one of those
very rare spots on Ocean Drive that I recommend, an
oasis among the desert of Tourist Traps populating
this once lovely street now turned into a monster of
mediocrity by greedy landlords and a city that could
use a heightened sensibility to appreciate what this
street cold have become.

LA MODERNA
1874 Bay Rd, Miami Beach, 786-717-7274
www.lamoderna-miami.com
CUISINE: Italian / Pizza
DRINKS: Full bar
SERVING: Lunch & Dinner
PRICE RANGE: $$
Trattoria offering a creative menu of Neapolitan pies and
rustic-modern pastas. Menu picks include: Spaghetti with
caviar and Oyster and crispy leeks. Great creative craft
cocktails.

LOS FUEGOS
Faena Hotel
3201 Collins Ave, Miami Beach, 786-655-5600
www.faena.com
CUISINE: Argentine
DRINKS: Full bar

SERVING: breakfast, lunch & dinner daily
PRICE RANGE: $$$$
NEIGHBORHOOD: Middle Beach
Located in one of the more elegant hotel properties in town, the Faena. There's a striking circular chandelier in the middle of the dining room with a hundred small lights that when working together create a masterful fixture. Then there's a bold sculpture of a unicorn on a pedestal in the other part of the place that, when I first saw it, brought to mind the Golden Calf made by
the Israelites when Moses went up to Mount Sinai. Looking around the Faena, the feeling creeps up on you that you're in the midst of over-the-top extravagance for which there is little excuse. (Not to be a party pooper.) There's an outdoor patio area with a bar where you can sit if the weather's good. Worth coming here for a drink just to take in the gorgeous interiors. South American eatery featuring seafood, steak and classic regional dishes of the Argentine. Impressive wine list (with eye-rolling prices to match). Favorites: 30oz bone-in ribeye with chimichurri and Seabass 'en Papillote'.

LUCALI
1930 Bay Rd, Miami Beach, 305-695-4441
www.lucalimenu.com
CUISINE: Italian
DRINKS: Full bar
SERVING: Dinner plus Lunch on Sat & Sun
PRICE RANGE: $$
NEIGHBORHOOD: Sunset Harbour
Nice little eatery serving brick-oven pizzas and salads. You can smell the wood they use in the oven—it's stacked up right by the bar. Bar offers Italian wines, craft draft and bottled beers. Pizzas are their specialty, but they also offer calzones, wings, meatballs, and desserts. Outdoor seating as well.

LURE FISHBAR
1601 Collins Ave, Miami Beach, 305-695-4550
Loews Hotel
www.lurefishbar.com
CUISINE: Seafood/Sushi
DRINKS: Full bar
SERVING: Dinner
PRICE RANGE: $$$
Located in the Loews Hotel, everything is nautical-themed from the décor to the cocktails. Classic seafood menu offering great surf 'n' turf, sushi, and oysters. Try their tasty signature crafted cocktails (most have at least six ingredients). Save room for their delicious Key Lime Pie made with house-made Graham Cracker and roasted white chocolate.

MACCHIALINA TAVERNA RUSTICA
820 Alton Rd., Miami Beach: 305-534-2124
www.macchialina.com
CUISINE: Italian
DRINKS: Full bar
SERVING: Dinner
This intimate (maybe 50 seats inside, with some on the street outside) eatery serves top-notch Italian fare including great dishes like Eggplant & Mozzarella and Wagyu Carpaccio. While the food is undeniably good, everything on the menu is $10 less at **Oliver's** just around the corner. (Of course, the food at Oliver's is a peg or two or even three down in quality than this gourmet place.) And the wine list here is not very friendly. I don't remember a single bottle under $50. Not cool. But I still come here often because I love it. (I just don't order wine.) The vibe here is one of the coolest in town. And trust me, it's ALWAYS packed. When I go, I arrive promptly when

they open at 6 so I can grab a seat and eat at the bar. Fills up fast. $$$

MARE MIO
447 Espanola Way, 305-397-8950
www.maremiorestaurant.com
WEBSITE DOWN AT PRESSTIME
CUISINE: Seafood
DRINKS: Full Bar
SERVING: Lunch & Dinner
PRICE RANGE: $$
Located on the historic Spanish street, this cute little eatery offers a creative seafood centric menu. Favorites: Grilled cuttlefish & black ink risotto and Seafood linguini. Fish is very fresh here.

MATADOR ROOM
Edition Hotel
2901 Collins Ave, Miami Beach, 786-257-4600
www.matadorroom.com
CUISINE: Spanish/Caribbean
DRINKS: Full Bar
SERVING: Dinner, Late Night
PRICE RANGE: $$$
This upscale eatery offers Jean-Georges Vongerichten's take on Latin cuisine, with some dishes copied from the chef's ABC Cocina in New York. Here you can dine on a seasonal menu of small and large plates. Beautiful oval dining room and bar that overlooks the pool. Menu picks include: Grilled Octopus and Short Ribs. Creative cocktails. The best thing about this place is that it's located off the stunning hotel lobby. I hadn't expected all that white marble. The way they up-lighted the potted palm to get the fronds to cast muted shadows on the white ceiling gave the place a very modern take on a noir look from the 1930s or '40s. Superior design concept, I must say. The

hotel bar is expensive and boring, to my taste, and the restaurant also is stuffy and shrug-inducing, requiring an effort. On the weekends, the place is packed as party-goers head to the **Basement** nightclub downstairs.

MISTER 01
1680 Michigan Ave, Miami Beach, 305-397-8189
www.mistero1.com
CUISINE: Pizza
DRINKS: Beer & Wine
SERVING: Lunch and Dinner
PRICE RANGE: $$
NEIGHBORHOOD: Lincoln Road
A popular pizza spot that takes reservations, believe it or not. Neapolitan-style pies, antipasti and salads. Small bare-bones eatery but the pizza is the best. Try the Nutella pizza for a real treat. Vegetarian options.

MONTY'S SUNSET
300 Alton Rd, Miami Beach, 305-672-1148
www.montyssobe.com
CUISINE: Seafood

DRINKS: Full Bar
SERVING: Lunch & Dinner
PRICE RANGE: $$
NEIGHBORHOOD: South Beach
This is about the only place you can go for lunch and use the pool. It's right on the water facing the Third Street Marina, so you get to see all the boats tied up on the docks. Large outdoor tiki hut bar attracts a big crowd. Popular waterfront seafood eatery with a raw bar & the usual fish shack fare. Besides the Stone crabs this place features live music, DJs, TVs for sports and happy hour special. Favorites: Lobster bisque, grouper tacos and Fried Shrimp. Another plus is the Free Parking – a rarity on South Beach.

MR. CHOW
W South Beach Hotel
2201 Collins Ave., 305-695-1695
www.mrchow.com
CUISINE: Chinese
DRINKS: Full bar
SERVING: Dinner nightly
The food's very nice, as a rule, but of course it ought to be. Can't go wrong with the Beijing chicken, the famous green prawns, whatever lobster dish they're serving, and my favorite: the crispy beef and duck. (Oh, and get the

fried rice.) They've gone all-out on the décor, and worth a trip just to see the place.

MY CEVICHE
235 Washington Ave., Miami Beach: 305-397-8710
www.myceviche.com
CUISINE: Seafood, Peruvian
DRINKS: No Alcohol
SERVING: Lunch, Dinner
It's a little hole-in-the wall but co-owners Roger Duarte and James Beard Award-nominated chef Sam Gorenstein are serving delicious ceviche. Everybody I know who loves ceviche LOVES this place. Very cheap, too. $$

NAIYARA
1854 Bay Rd, Miami Beach, 786-275-6005
www.naiyara.com
CUISINE: Thai/Japanese
DRINKS: Full bar
SERVING: Dinner
PRICE RANGE: $$$
Popular eatery serving up a creative menu of Thai street food, sushi and Asian specialties. Favorites include: Crispy bok choy, Chicken dumplings, and Creamy ramen noodle soup with prawns. Unique cocktails. Reservations recommended.

NAUTILUS CABANA CLUB
Nautilus Hotel
1825 Collins Ave, Miami Beach, 786-483-2650
www.arlohotels.com
CUISINE: Latin American
DRINKS: Full Bar
SERVING: Breakfast, Lunch & Dinner
PRICE RANGE: $$

Beachside eatery with a menu of seafood-focused Mediterranean fare & vegetarian options. Favorites: Steak and fish, Tzatziki and vegetables. Often, they have live music. Great choice for Brunch.

NEWS CAFE $$

800 Ocean Dr.; 305-538-6397
CUISINE: American, a little Middle Eastern
DRINKS: Full bar
SERVING: 24 hours
www.newscafe.com.
Wide variety of American and some so-so Mediterranean dishes. Yep, this is the place Versace had breakfast before being shot. You can, too! (Have breakfast, that is.) Whenever I come here, I go as early in the morning as possible – this is the only time Ocean Drive is not surging with a hoard of tourists. You can hear birds sing. You can smell the fresh morning air. You can really *experience* South Beach the way it was when it was great.

OLIVER'S BISTRO

959 West Ave., Miami Beach: 305-535-3050
CUISINE: American (some Italian)
DRINKS: Full bar
SERVING: breakfast, lunch & dinner daily. (Opens at 9)
www.oliversmiamibeach.com
One of the nicest places frequented by locals. Staff is courteous, the food superior, and their excellent chef, Ed Malloy, hasn't allowed the kitchen to fall off the high standards he set when they first opened. In good weather, you can sit outside and watch the locals stroll by on West Avenue.

Starters: We like the Shrimp & Brie Quesadilla, enhanced with sour cream, black bean relish, salsa and the expected guacamole. Yum. Also, we favor the Smoked Salmon & Brie Crostini. Full range of salads, from

Crunchy Chicken to a very nice Cobb; Greek Salad with Grilled Calamari; Spicy Beef Salad. A lovely Rare Seared Sushi Grade Ahi Tuna Niciose Salad is a winner, too.

Main course favorites: quite a few pasta and risotto dishes stand out, from as simple as you can get (Linguini Aglio e Olio or Spaghetti & Meatballs). Steak frites platter is good. One of my favorite things here is to order the mussels with spicy sausage in a tomato garlic broth and have them toss a side of pasta into it: for about $20 you get a great meal, half of which you can take home. (They use Italian sausage in the dish instead of the chorizo you get everywhere else in town, making the dish much, much more flavorful.)

Serves "late breakfast" till 2:30 daily, and has a full brunch menu on weekends. Also has a very nice Vegetable Plate. $$$

PAPI STEAK
736 1st St, Miami Beach, 305-800-PAPI
http://papisteak.com/
CUISINE: Steakhouse
DRINKS: Full Bar
SERVING: Dinner
PRICE RANGE: $$$$
NEIGHBORHOOD: SoFi (South of Fifth)
Intimate dining featuring classic dishes and prime meats. They're offering something a little more subdued and civilized than the circus you have to endure at nearby Prime 112 (although big shot Latin American blowhards with their hookers can be seen here as well). The interior is quite dramatic, with highly colorful wall treatments over the plush red velvet banquettes. Specialty cocktails and impressive wine list. Most items are big enough to share. (So is the bill, LOL!) Favorites: Papi Steak (a huge ribeye) and Latkes with crème fraiche.

PARRILLA LIBERTY & PIZZA
1255 Washington Ave.; 305-532-7599
CUISINE: Argentine
DRINKS: beer & wine
SERVING: Daily noon – midnight
www.laparrillaliberty.com. A
All the favorites from Argentina but cheap, cheap, cheap!
(A little more chewy than great meat, but still… don't eat
here if you have dentures.) $

PLANTA
850 Commerce St, Miami Beach, 305-397-8513
www.plantarestaurants.com
CUISINE: Vegetarian
DRINKS: Full bar
SERVING: Breakfast & Brunch, Lunch, Dinner
PRICE RANGE: $$$$
NEIGHBORHOOD: SoFi (South of Fifth)
Just a few feet from Joe's Stone Crab, across from Joe's
self-parking lot, is this Vegetarian eatery that's well worth
your time. This is most certainly NOT your typical
Vegetarian spot, but very high-end, with a creative menu
that is equal to the stunning interiors they've got to offer
here. Lots of high windows and skylight treatment. I eat

veggies every day, but I seldom order vegetarian because the food is usually so uninspired. Not so here. offering an impressive menu featuring flatbreads, croquettes, and steamed dumplings. Try the Buffalo cauliflower pizza. The Crispy Chicken sandwich, for instance, is made with buttermilk fried cauliflower, daikon, carrot, cilantro, challah bun, tajin fries. You won't believe how good it tastes. Reservations recommended.

PRIME ONE TWELVE
112 Ocean Dr. (The Browns Hotel), 305-532-8112
www.mylesrestaurantgroup.com
CUISINE: Steakhouse
DRINKS: Full bar
SERVING: Lunch from 11:30 weekdays, dinner from 6:30. NEIGHBORHOOD: SoFi (South of Fifth)
Basketball players and other celebs come here to see, be seen, and order the 48 oz. Porterhouse. If you want to go here but not "go there," go for lunch at the bar and order a sandwich and a beer. There's an appetizer here, the truffled deviled eggs with caviar for $20 that ought to be

tried before you die. (In fact, this dish will HELP you die, but you'll go down smiling!) Oh, just a warning: this will be the MOST EPENSIVE place for lunch or dinner you can go on South Beach. I can't think of anywhere more ridiculously priced. *Tip:* Miles, the guy that owns this place, also owns a busy diner popular with locals (like me) right around the corner on Second Street, called **BIG PINK**. Of course, you don't get the big prime steaks, it's diner food, but the quality is great, the portions huge and the prices much less draconian. (Those same famous jocks also go to Big Pink, by the way.)

QUALITY MEATS
1501 Collins Ave, Miami Beach, 305-340-3333
www.qualitymeatsmiami.com
CUISINE: Steakhouse/American (New)
DRINKS: Full Bar
SERVING: Dinner
PRICE RANGE: $$$
A Miami location of the famous NYC chophouse, this dining room is located in a historic Art Deco Hotel. Executive chef Craig Koketsu offers a creative menu of classic cuts of beef, not that South Beach needed another steakhouse. Still, this place is a lot of fun—busy, lively, noisy, fun. Menu picks include: Short Ribs and Double tomahawk rib steak. Some items are a little odd: a thick slice of bacon served with peanut butter and a relish including jalapenos. Wow! Most steakhouses carry the same tired old side dishes, but here at Quality Meats, there are some interesting selections, like the creamed corn (out of this world) or the roasted trumpet mushrooms, or the crispy potatoes served in a skillet—when the waiter brings it, he will pour a garlic-herb butter on top. This would make a meal in itself, and one that would be completely satisfying. This place offers a great dining experience with an old world feel.

SARDINIA-ENOTECA RISTORANTE $$$

1801 Purdy Ave, 305-531-2228
CUISINE: Italian-Sardinian
DRINKS: Full bar
SERVING: Daily noon – midnight
www.sardinia-ristorante.com

Look over the menu online. This is Sardinian, *not* Italian. I love the little cheese and meat boards where they let you mix and match cheeses with meats. The side dishes (roasted beets, braised baby Brussels sprouts) are great. My favorite starter is sautéed chicken livers with fava beans. A meal by itself. (The wines are from Sardinia too, but tend to be lighter than the best Italian wines, but they're eminently quaffable.)

SCARPETTA

Fontainebleau
4441 Collins Ave, 305-674-4660 / 305-538-2000
www.fontainebleau.com/web/dining/scarpetta
CUISINE: Italian
DRINKS: Full bar
SERVING: Dinner daily from 5:30.
NEIGHBORHOOD: Middle Beach

There's no question that when this dowager hotel reopened after a renovation that costs tens of millions of dollars (2010), this was the prize jewel of all the well-hyped restaurants. When you arrive at the hotel, they will have to tell you how to get there, it's so far away from where an Uber will drop you. (And I had to stop twice to ask directions.) When you get to the space, you'll find it's just the opposite of what you expected: a small, intimate, charmingly decorated room that feels like it's anywhere but here. The food is nothing short of spectacular. You've never had pasta that was this delicate, unless you've been to Chef Scott Conant's eatery in New York. It's the same great food. Favorite starters are the crispy fritto misto and the creamy polenta. There's also a Japanese mackerel tartar that jumps right out at you. Bypass the steaks, chops and seafood and focus on his pasta dishes as your entrée, especially the scialatelli and the agnolotti dal plin. You'll go nuts. Don't miss the Osso Bucco.

SEGAFREDO ESPRESSO
1040 Lincoln Rd.; 305-673-0047
http://www.sze-originale.com/
CUISINE: Café, Appetizers
DRINKS: Full bar
SERVING: lunch & dinner daily
I don't recommend but 3 or 4 places on all of Lincoln Road, for a good reason—the restaurants here are almost as much of an unmitigated rip-off as the terrible places you find on Ocean Drive. This one, however, is different. The aim here is to reflect the lifestyle of Italy's famously fun and charming coffee bars. It's hard to beat the ambience here – lounging on a sofa out on Lincoln Road with a coffee or a drink or a meal. The food is very reasonably priced and the quality is very exception. I know the owner quite well, and when I go to Lincoln Road, I invariably drop in here. There's a tiny bar inside where you can often get a seat if it's packed outside. (That's where you'll find me.) The colorful fountain is by famed Cuban artist Carlos Alves. $$$

SMITH & WOLLENSKY
1 Washington Ave.; 305-673-2800
www.smithandwollensky.com
CUISINE: American, Steakhouse, Seafood
DRINKS: Full bar
SERVING: lunch and dinner daily
NEIGHBORHOOD: SoFi (South of Fifth)
Sorry, but no visit to South Beach is complete without
dropping by this place, even if it's for a drink at the
outside bar overlooking Gov't Cut where you can see the
boat traffic coming into and out of the Port of Miami.
They have a cold seafood platter that's killer, and the
million-dollar view is free!

SPIGA
1228 Collins Ave, Miami Beach, 305-534-0079
www.spigarestaurant.com
CUISINE: Italian / Seafood
DRINKS: Beer & Wine Only
SERVING: Dinner
PRICE RANGE: $$$
I tend to forget about this intimate eatery offers a menu of
Northern Italian cuisine including great seafood and
homemade pastas. Why? Because it's tucked inside the

lobby of the tiny and elegant Impala Hotel. It's been here for years and I just love it. Outdoor garden dining. Nice wine list.

STILTSVILLE FISH BAR
1787 Purdy Ave, Miami Beach, 786-353-0477
www.stiltsvillefishbar.com
CUISINE: Seafood, Tapas/Small Plates, Cocktail Bars
DRINKS: Full Bar
SERVING: Dinner, Lunch & Dinner Sat - Sun
PRICE RANGE: $$$-$$$$
Casual eatery featuring big open garage style window/doors. It's a lot less hectic and bustling during the week, while on weekends, it's one of "the" places to be. Without a reservation on the weekends, you'll get turned away. As "rustic" as they've tried to make this place, there's nothing rustic about the food. It's smart, sophisticated, expertly prepared—everything. Creative menu offering fresh options from fish to vegetables. The fish is delivered daily from fishermen working in Key Largo, Key West and here in Miami. Very fish-centric menu. The leftover fish parts are smoked to make a very nice dip which you ought to get as a starter for the whole table to sample. A popular dish is the whole fried snapper. (Don't worry about forgetting this—the waiters push it, actually.) It's visually striking when it lands on your table. Impressive salads. Favorites: Shrimp 'N Grits and Lobster Mac N' Mushrooms. The chef is noted for his fried chicken (which he debuted at **Yardbird** over near Lincoln Road). But don't get it—it's far too expensive. (Instead, get the fried chicken next time you're at **Joe's Stone Crab**—you'll get a half chicken for what it costs for a single piece here.) Dining room includes bar (with perhaps the most uncomfortable bar stools in all Christendom) and lounge area.

STUBBORN SEED

101 Washington Ave, Miami Beach, 786-322-5211
www.stubbornseed.com
101 Washington Ave., Miami Beach
CUISINE: American (New)/Seafood
DRINKS: Full Bar
SERVING: Dinner; closed Mondays
PRICE RANGE: $$$-$$$$
NEIGHBORHOOD: SoFi (South of Fifth)
Opened by Top Chef 13 winner Jeremy Ford. This very
small eatery offers a menu of seasonal American cuisine
created by a master at his craft. Tip: Try the Chef's
Tasting Menu which has some of the menu's best.
Favorites: Smoked foie gras, Maine Lobster poached in
butter, lavash (chicken liver butter), warm celery root, and
the Slow Cooked Florida Snapper. Craft cocktails. I hope
to God this place stays open more than a year. I almost
skipped putting this place in my book because so many of
this "type" of place never make it. The food is so good I
am praying. Yes, the portions are small and the prices are
steep, but still... this place is a superior achievement. I
don't think the name helps, but as long as he keeps
cooking the way he's cooking, I don't give a damn what
he calls it.

SUGAR FACTORY

Hotel Victor, 1144 Ocean Dr, Miami Beach, 917-327-
8096
www.sugarfactory.com/miami
CUISINE: American (New) / Desserts
DRINKS: Full bar
SERVING: Breakfast, Lunch & Dinner
PRICE RANGE: $$
Located in the beautiful art deco Hotel Victor, this newly-
redecorated 3,000 square foot brasserie offers a candy
shop up front and patio dining overlooking Ocean Drive

and the ocean. Known for their world-famous Couture Pops, creative cocktails, the menu also offers pancakes, crepes, salads, burgers, and creative desserts.

Thomas Keller hard at work

SURF CLUB RESTAURANT
9011 Collins Ave., Surfside, 305-768-9440
www.surfclubrestaurant.com
CUISINE: American (Traditional)/Modern European
DRINKS: Full bar
SERVING: Dinner
PRICE RANGE: $$$$
NEIGHBORHOOD: North Beach / Bal Harbour
World-class dining specializing in meats. This is Thomas Keller's spot in what used to be the old private Surf Club, a bastion of "society" since the 1930s. Winston Churchill set up his easel and painted some watercolors here. This place was built in the old club house, and across the high-ceilinged hallway is another restaurant, **Le Sirenuse**, which I like better than this Keller spot. If you're coming

to dinner here, arrive early and have a drink in the spacious bar across in Le Sirenuse—the architectural details in this space (in the Spanish-Moorish, Mediterranean Revival Robber Baron Style of Addison Mizner) are well worth seeing. Favorites: Rib eye with Foie Gras; the short ribs (braised 48-hours); and Hokkaido scallops. Roasted chicken is prepared and served table-side. (It's flavorful & juicy.) The famous Beef Wellington is so rich you might want to throw up after eating it, though it's a work of art if you can handle it. Delicious desserts.

Bar at Le Sirenuse

SUSHI BY BOU
Versace Villa
1116 Ocean Dr, Miami Beach, 305-922-9195
www.sushibybou.com
CUISINE: Japanese/Sushi
DRINKS: Full bar
SERVING: Dinner
PRICE RANGE: $$$$
NEIGHBORHOOD: Ocean Drive
You'll walk up the front steps where the designer Versace was gunned down as he tried to enter his villa back in

86

1997. On the top floor of the mansion is this intimate counter with only a half dozen seats. Private chef serves. Fresh sushi and creative cocktails. Amazing experience if you want to impress someone. Price includes 17 piece omakase meal. Take a stroll around the interior of Versace's mansion while you're here. I went to quite a few parties in this place when Versace was alive, and it still retains some of the magical excesses of those days (except the people are not as sexy and attractive as they were then). Still quite a sight.

SWEET LIBERTY DRINKS & SUPPLY COMPANY
237-B 20th St, Miami Beach, 305-763-8217
www.mysweetliberty.com
CUISINE: American (New)
DRINKS: Beer & Wine Only
SERVING: Dinner, Brunch on Sundays
PRICE RANGE: $$
NEIGHBORHOOD: Convention Center
Near the Bass Museum and the renovated Convention Center is this hideaway known and frequented by every serious bartender in Miami because it (well, original boss, here, Lermayer) gets credit for spawning the "craft cocktail" trend in Miami. The bartenders here *really* know their shit. It's very unassuming, even down market, but they have cheap oysters during happy hour, and VERY reasonable prices for food. (Cocktails are not outrageously priced.) Favorites: Lobster rolls, fried chicken and Cauliflower nachos. Happy hour specials. A pool table for those interested. Lermayer once said, "The cocktail is America's first epicurean contribution to the world." And unlike all those other places where they serve "craft cocktails," here you'll find no velvet rope and (for Miami) a refreshing absence of bullshit and attitude.

TANUKI
1080 Alton Rd, Miami Beach, 305-615-1055
www.tanukimiami.com
CUISINE: Asian Fusion, Dim Sum, Japanese
DRINKS: Full Bar
SERVING: Dinner only on Monday & Tues, Lunch &
Dinner Wed - Sun
PRICE RANGE: $$$
Upscale eatery specializing in sushi, dim sum and wok
with some of the finest Japanese, Thai, Korean, Malaysian
and Chinese dishes. Favorites: Dim sum and Shanghainese
soup dumplings. For a special occasion try their Peking
Duck. Great desserts.

TIME OUT MARKET
1601 Drexel Ave, Miami Beach, 786-753-5388
www.timeoutmarket.com
CUISINE: Food Hall
DRINKS: Full bar
SERVING: Lunch & Dinner
PRICE RANGE: $$-$$$
NEIGHBORHOOD: Lincoln Road
Upscale food hall (the original is in Lisbon) with 18
eateries under one roof – everything from Vegan, Pho,
Cuban, Mexican, Italian to Cuban ice cream. Two
celebrity chefs, Norman Van Aken and Jeremy Ford, also
have booths. Bar is in the center, shared by everyone.
Prices are a little high and a lot of locals don't come here
for that reason, but the place is fun. Big screen TV, Live
DJ on weekends. Indoor/outdoor seating.

UNDER THE MANGO TREE
737 Fifth St, 786-558-5103
www.mangotreemiami.com
CUISINE: Juice Bars/Smoothies/Acai Bowls
DRINKS: No Booze

SERVING: 8 a.m. – 6 p.m.
PRICE RANGE: $$
Small counter-serve juice bar with a selection of veggie snacks and sandwiches. Favorites: Marley Acai Bowl and Spicy Kale Melt. Impressive juice selection. Eco-friendly gift items.

UPLAND MIAMI
49 Collins Ave, Miami Beach, 305-602-9998
www.uplandmiami.com
CUISINE: American (New)
DRINKS: Beer & Wine Only
SERVING: Dinner, Lunch Sat & Sun
PRICE RANGE: $$$
NEIGHBORHOOD: SoFi (South of Fifth)
This chic NYC spin-off with fine dining is just a block from the beach, but it's sophisticated and casual at the same time. Bright and cheerful place. It offers a creative menu of wood-fired dishes with Californian & Italian influences. Favorites: Salmon, Wood roasted beets, wood fired Florida prawns, dry-aged bone-in New York strip and Tuscan-Style Lamb Chops. I always get the crispy squash blossoms to start. Bartenders are well trained, too. Nice wine selection. Has a bar with 6 or 7 seats where you can eat if you're by yourself. Chef Justin Smillie comes from Upland, Calif., which explains the name of this place.

VIA EMILIA 9
1120 15th St, Miami Beach,786-216-7150
www.viaemilia9.com
CUISINE: Italian
DRINKS: Beer & Wine Only
SERVING: Lunch & Dinner
PRICE RANGE: $$
NEIGHBORHOOD: near Lincoln Road

This is one of those little "finds" you read guidebooks like this to discover. You'd never stumble onto it by yourself. Just a half-block east of Alton Road is this Italian eatery with a menu of authentic Italian classics and house made Perezpasta. You'll see the Chef Wendy Cacciatori behind the counter cooking almost every night. The place is split into 2 rooms, a diner-counter on one side (behind which he cooks) and am intimate, charming romantic room on the other side of the wall where candlelight flickers on the little tables. (I prefer to sit in the brighter diner side just because I love to watch this guy cook.) His concept was simple when he came to South Beach—he'd only cook dishes you could get on the via Emilia in Italy that happens to run through towns like Bologna, Parma and Modena. If you can't get to Italy anytime soon, you're in luck. Come here. Favorites: Eggplant parmigiana and gnocchi. Well, any of the pastas. They're all great. Nice wine list. Reservations recommended on weekends, when it fills with locals.

VILLA AZUR RESTAURANT & LOUNGE
309 - 23rd St., Miami Beach: 305-763-8688
www.villaazurmiami.com
CUISINE: Italian, Mediterranean
DRINKS: Full Bar
SERVING: Dinner
Went here on my birthday last year. And immediately returned again and again. A bit of French Riviera elegance in South Beach serving delicious dishes like seared tuna with avocado and baby spinach. Actress Halle Berry's boyfriend is one of the owners. A favorite of celebrities and fashionistas. $$$$

MIDDLE & NORTH BEACHES
(from 30th Street in Miami Beach up through Bal Harbour, Surfside, Aventura)
& MIAMI NORTH

This section includes everything in the County north from (and including) the 79th Street Causeway (on the beach side), the northern part of Miami Beach, the few restaurants on the Causeway; Bal Harbour and Bay Harbor. On the mainland, it includes Miami Shores north to the town of North Miami and the inaccurately named City of North Miami Beach (it has no beach and is a hideous, relentlessly tacky part of this town) up to Aventura, where you'll find a few nice places.

CAFÉ AVANTI
732 – 41st St., Miami Beach: 305-538-4400
CUISINE: Italian
DRINKS: full bar
SERVING: L weekdays; D nightly.
www.cafeavanti.com
Frequented by locals who love the food. It's the perfect cozy spot that makes traditional dishes even better than any Italian Grandma. I go there specifically for the linguini con Vongole (they use 2 dozen tender clams in this dish). They also carry the Delaplaine fine sparkling wine from Napa. Save room for the dessert cart. **Jessica**, the owner's daughter, is the hostess with the mostess. There's plenty of parking on the street and a "private" back door entrance. $$$

CARPACCIO
Bal Harbour Shops, 9700 Collins Ave., Bal Harbour: 305-867-7777
www.carpaccioatbalharbour.com

CUISINE: Italian; DRINKS: full bar; SERVING: lunch, dinner

I get up here about 3 or 4 times a year. I sit at the bar because at the tables you're surrounded by the "ladies who lunch" crowd who come up here to shop. The hustle and bustle of the place is fun because you feel like you're in New York. (Often, waiters forget to tell you the specials. Ask for them. I almost never order off the menu any more. The specials are always that good.) $$$

HAKKASAN
Fontainebleau, 4441 Collins Ave., Miami Beach: 786-276-1388
www.hakkasan.com
CUISINE: Chinese
DRINKS: full bar
SERVING: nightly from 6; *dim sum* lunch weekends, 12-3.

I must say that Chinese food has always been Chinese food to me. By that, I mean the concept of "gourmet" Chinese food has similarly seemed to me like a misnomer. But years ago I went to a place in London and then a place down in Miami called Christine Lee's, and my opinion changed instantly. When it's done right, there is no better food than Chinese, and Hakkasan proves the point. Anything you select from the extensive menu will please. But I'm partial to the crisp-skinned roasted duck. I have to have it every trip. $$$$

LA CÔTE
Fontainebleau, 4441 Collins Ave., Miami Beach: 305-674-4710
www.fontainebleau.com
CUISINE: American; some European
DRINKS: full bar
SERVING: lunch, early dinner (till 7 p.m.)

www.fontainebleau.com

Flatbreads, salads, sandwiches. Second floor of the pool
deck at this famous hotel. A great place to look over the
ocean. Believe it or not, most of the places you can eat in
the hotels lining the water don't have water views,
obstructed as they are by sand dunes, sea oats, berms, and
other manmade obstacles. But here, you're above it all.

LE ZOO
BAL HARBOUR SHOPS
9700 Collins Ave, 305-602-9663
www.lezoo.com
CUISINE: French
DRINKS: Beer & Wine Only
SERVING: Lunch & Dinner
PRICE RANGE: $$$
NEIGHBORHOOD: Bal Harbour

Popular brasserie with an authentic French feel. It's like
sitting on the sidewalk at a Parisian café. Except you're
surrounded by the upscale shops like Prada, Chanel and
Saks. It's right next door to the old standby that's been in
Bal Harbour for decades, Carpaccio. But I always choose
this place over Carpaccio. It's located right at the valet, so
you're in for a treat if you like to look at expensive cars.
Aston Martins, Bugattis, Lamborghinis, Rolls Royces, you
name it. There's a small indoor section, but it's more fun
to sit outside. Menu of French classics. Favorites: Veal
Piccata and Steak Tartare Du Parc. Though I've had
everything on the menu, I gravitate toward the steak frites
more often than not. The shoestring fries are expertly
cooked. (If they have cucumber soup the day you visit, for
God's sake get it. So refreshing and flavorful. I could
drink this stuff by the gallon.) Great cocktails and an
impressive wine list.

NOBU
4525 Collins Ave., 305-695-3232
www.noburestaurants.com
CUISINE: Japanese
DRINKS: Full bar
SERVING: dinner nightly
South Beach branch of Chef Nobu Matsuhisa's Japanese
empire. Among the cold dishes (these are all appetizers),
love the yellowtail sashimi with tiny slices of Jalapeno
(hot!); salmon kelp roll; sea urchin tiradito; yellowfin tuna
tataki; and the monkfish pate with caviar. Standouts
among hot starters include their famous rock shrimp
tempura; Alaskan king crab tempura; Tasmanian ocean
trout with crispy baby spinach. Wide range of Kushiyaki

and Tobanyaki specialties as well as the usual sushi and sashimi selections a la carte.

THE PALM
9650 E. Bay Harbor Dr., Bay Harbor Islands: 305-868-7256
CUISINE: steakhouse
DRINKS: full bar
SERVING: dinner from 5
www.thepalm.com
Yes, this is the same Palm as the one in New York. Same menu. Same everything. Still the best steaks anywhere, and all those super side dishes everybody else has copied. Bay Harbor is reached by going north on Collins Avenue. Take a left at 96th Street and go west over the bridge into the little island town of Bay Harbor. Take the first right. It's there on the left. I remember this place when it was called the Post & Paddock. A great room. Worth a trip. $$$$

SAND BAR + KITCHEN
6752 Collins Ave., Miami Beach, 305-397-8675
https://sandbarkitchen.com/
CUISINE: American / premium quality

DRINKS: full bar; big selection of craft beers
SERVING: lunch and dinner
PRICE RANGE: $$
NEIGHBORHOOD: North Beach
Though it may look like a sports bar, with a couple of
dozen monitors hanging on the walls, there's a LOT more
to this place than meets the eye. And that secret is in the
kitchen, where owner Timmy Wilcox and his team churn
out some of the best food served in Miami, from the tuna
tartare to the smoked ribs (he has baby backs, St. Louis
style, and also great brisket) and chicken that he smokes
himself every day or so in a little smoker out on the back
patio. The pulled pork sandwich is superior, as is all the
food. Mexican street corn, Sandbar Nachos (Refried beans,
pico de gallo, cheddar sauce, guacamole, sour cream; add
chili, grilled chicken or shrimp), great chicken wings with
choice of 6 sauces. Bigger plates like steaks and lamb
chops also of the highest quality. He recently added an
excellent New Orleans style gumbo to the menu. Drink
specials during games, happy hour, pool table, darts. Well
worth a stop.

Pork belly fried buns at Sand Bar + Kitchen

This section includes the hot new restaurant area **"Midtown,"** which is separated from the **Design District** by 36th Street. To the north of 36th Street is the Design District; to the south, Midtown.

Wynwood is just to the south of Midtown.

The **Biscayne Corridor** runs from Downtown up along a seedy but slowly improving Biscayne Boulevard until you hit the Miami Shores area, where things die down.

You'll find a lot of cheap restaurants ($ and $$) here because it's not about tourists, it's about locals.

1-800 LUCKY
143 NW 23rd St, Miami, 305-768-9826
https://www.1800lucky.com/
CUISINE: Asian Fusion
DRINKS: Full bar
SERVING: Lunch
NEIGHBORHOOD: Wynwood
PRICE RANGE: $$-$$$
Food court with an "Industrial look" offering several eateries serving food focused on Asian cuisine – everything from ramen to sushi. Communal tables. Ice cream served outside. Live DJ nights/weekends, when it gets really crowded. Indoor/Outdoor seating. Free Wi-Fi. Pet-friendly.

1111 PERUVIAN BISTRO
1111 SW 1st Ave, #106-D, Miami, 786-615-9633

www.1111peruvianbistro.com/
CUISINE: Peruvian
DRINKS: Full bar
SERVING: Lunch & Dinner; closed Sun
PRICE RANGE: $$$
NEIGHBORHOOD: Midtown
Sleek modern eatery offering Peruvian specialties with
Asian twists. Popular dishes like ceviche, tiraditos, King
crab and Poached chicken causa. High quality food.

ALTER
223 NW 23rd St, Miami, 305-573-5996 / **Wynwood**
www.altermiami.com
CUISINE: American (New)
DRINKS: Full Bar
SERVING: Lunch (till 2:30) & Dinner (from 7) Tues-Sat;
closed Sun & Mon.
PRICE RANGE: $$$
Modern new eatery offering a menu of refined and creative
New American cuisine. One of the hottest restaurants in all
of Miami. No white tablecloths, just plain wooden tables
and stark wooden chairs. Very trendy, but don't hold that
against the place, because the food pouring out of the open
kitchen is most certainly up to snuff. Menu picks include:
Rock Shrimp roll; Eggplant "pastrami" (I know what it
sounds like, just try it); deboned chicken stuffed with
ground up thigh meat & foie gras; luscious prawns served
over grits and topped with chorizo oil, mole and
huitlacoche cream. (You won't find this kind of "shrimp &
grits" in Atlanta or Charleston!) Wonderful place. Very
exciting. (But to be completely honest, half the people I
bring here hate the place, finding the food presentation to
be highly pretentious. You'll get a soup bowl the size of a
Frisbee with a tiny little spoonful of soup in it. That sort of
thing. Needless to say, the chef has won almost every
award you can possibly win.)

BEAKER & GRAY

2637 N. Miami Ave, Miami 305-699-2637
www.beakerandgray.com
CUISINE: Modern American/Tapas
DRINKS: Full bar
SERVING: Lunch/Dinner; Dinner only on Sat & Sun
PRICE RANGE: $$
NEIGHBORHOOD: **Wynwood**
This is a cool hot spot near my warehouse (where we keep
our wine) and studio (where I write my books). Everybody
loves it. The guys here have joined forces to create this
innovative eatery offering internationally inspired
American fare. While you might have heard of the items
on the menu, the way they add their own little twists make
everything very distinctive and unique, from the Cuban
croquettas to the Chicken fingers, Pumpkin gnocchi and
cauliflower. Indoor and outdoor seating.

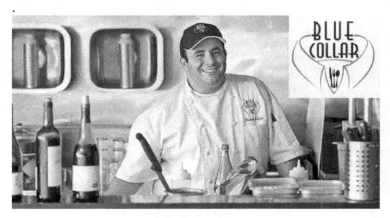

BLUE COLLAR

6730 Biscayne Blvd., Miami: 305-756-0366 / **Biscayne Corridor**
www.bluecollarmiami.com
CUISINE: American

DRINKS: Beer & Wine
SERVING: Lunch, Dinner, Brunch
One of my favorite places in Miami. Chef Danny Serfer and his talented team, working out of a rundown motel on Biscayne, have created one of the "go-to" places in Miami, frequented by highbrow and lowbrow alike. They dish up American comfort food in a small comfortable setting. Pork & Beans, Shrimp & Grits, Braised Brisket, Chicken Cordon Bleu, all worth ordering. One of the things I like about this place is the blackboard listing about 20 vegetable dishes prepared creatively: you can choose 4 of them for $19. Curried cauliflower, grilled asparagus with a blue cheese vinaigrette, warm potato salad with bacon. You get the idea. A meal by itself. Plan on sharing. Delicious desserts. $$

.

ENRIQUETA'S SANDWICH SHOP
186 NE 29th St, Miami: 305-573-4681 /
http://enriquetas.com
CUISINE: Cuban
DRINKS: Beer/Wine
SERVING: Breakfast/Lunch till 3pm.

Really basic Cuban food. Fast, cheap and in the most interesting little spot. (I even put this place in my novel, *The Meter Maid Murders*—it's the place where the robbers stop to get a Cuban sandwich and café con leche.) Breakfast: two eggs, bacon or ham, Cuban toast, café con leche, and a cup of fresh squeezed orange juice, is less than McDonald's. Lunch is just as good and just as reasonable. Everybody in Miami has been here at one time or another. Power players from downtown, cops off the street, construction workers, the UPS driver. It's all locals, no tourists. Although Cubans aren't noted for their punctuality, this place closes promptly at 3, but if you get in by 3, you can order and they won't throw you out.

JIMMY'S EASTSIDE DINER
7201 Biscayne Blvd., Miami: 305-754-3692 / **Biscayne Corridor**
No web site
CUISINE: American/Diner
DRINKS: No Bar
SERVING: Breakfast/ Lunch
Although Jimmy's is your typical greasy spoon diner, the food is always really good. This diner has been around for a very long time, a favorite of locals. When they have it on the menu, try the lamb shank. Delicious. $

JOEY'S ITALIAN CAFÉ
2506 NW 2nd Ave, Miami: 305-438-0488 / **Wynwood**
www.joeyswynwood.com
CUISINE: Italian
DRINKS: Full Bar
SERVING: Lunch / Dinner
Always a lively crowd in this spot owned by Tony Goldman's son, Joey. Updated modern Italian cuisine. Consistently good. $$-$$$

KYU
251 NW 25th St, Miami, 786-577-0150
www.kyumiami.com
CUISINE: Asian Fusion
DRINKS: Full bar
SERVING: Lunch & Dinner; closed Mon
PRICE RANGE: $$
NEIGHBORHOOD: **Wynwood**
Modern hipster eatery with a great menu of Asian fare and creative cocktails. Favorites include: Butter Fried Chicken and Crispy Pork "Guy" (fried pork belly pieces – delicious). Great happy hour menu. Reservations recommended.

MIGNONETTE
210 NE 18th St (corner of 2nd Ave), Miami, 305-374-4635 / **Edgewwater**
www.mignonettemiami.com
CUISINE: American; oyster bar; seafood
DRINKS: Beer & Wine
SERVING: Lunch-Dinner-Brunch
NEIGHBORHOOD: Edgewater (just south of **Wynwood**)
Danny Serfer is famous in these parts for a restaurant further up Biscayne Boulevard, **Blue Collar**, where American comfort food has never been rendered more comfortably. Here, just 2 blocks off Biscayne, and right across the Causeway from South Beach, he has an oyster bar that also serves a wide variety of fresh seafood (from whole hog snapper to scallop crudo). When I go, I sit at the bar and choose from 10 or more oyster selections while drinking a nice Alsatian pinot blanc. (He's only a few blocks from my office.) I usually avoid things like fried clams on Miami menus. But when I tried them here, I realized he was making these dishes the way they would on Cape Cod. Better, even. Try the fried conch as well. By the way, across the street is one of the oldest cemeteries in

Miami, well worth a stroll through after stuffing yourself here.

MANDOLIN AEGEAN BISTRO

4312 NE 2nd Ave., Miami: 305-749-9140/ **Design District**

mandolinmiami.com

CUISINE: Greek, with some mixed Mediterranean

DRINKS: Beer/Wine

SERVING: Dinner

Intimate and cozy (and we mean intimate—it's in a small house) with great service and great food. Everybody raves about the white sangria, but it's not for me. (Wine for me.) I've tried almost every dish on the menu, and there's not a loser in the lot. Outdoors is nice in good weather. $-$$

MC KITCHEN

4141 NE 2nd Ave., Miami, 305-456-9948

www.mckitchenmiami.com

CUISINE: Italian

DRINKS: Full Bar

SERVING: Lunch-Dinner

PRICE RANGE: $$$

NEIGHBORHOOD: Design District

Another fine dining experience in the Design District, just a couple of blocks from pioneering Michael Schwartz's **Michael's Genuine**. Here it's Dena Marino, serving up some of the most prized Italian cuisine in Miami. Spinach lasagna, lovely burrata stuffed with roasted squash, charred octopus drenched in olive oil, spaghetti with shrimp—all are excellent. At lunch one day I had a bloody Mary that the waiter told me had ketchup in it. It sounded so terrible. But after tasting it, I ordered 2 more in rapid succession. (Service can be glacial, so tell them if you want things speeded up.)

103

MICHAEL'S GENUINE FOOD & DRINK
130 NE 40th St., Miami: 305- 573-5550 / **Design District**
www.michaelsgenuine.com
CUISINE: American
DRINKS: Full bar
SERVING: Lunch / Dinner
Simple décor, but you didn't come to this world-renowned
eatery for the décor. **Chef Michael Schwartz** (who rose to
some prominence on South Beach at the now closed
Nemo's) became an international culinary star when he
jumped over to the still-dormant Design District and
opened this place focusing on locally sourced ingredients.
Menu changes as he sees fit (and I'm glad he saw fit to
change it recently, because it had been a while), but you
can't go wrong with anything you get here. I even get the
chicken here. Plain, simple chicken, which I rarely eat in
restaurants because it's usually so incredibly awful. Here,
though, it's moist and juicy. Indoor-outdoor. Hard to get in
during peak times, even in summer! I always sneak in
early, where I usually eat at the bar helping myself
liberally from the bowls of radishes they offer). Great
staff. Well-balanced wine list, if a bit heavy on the obscure
German selections. $$$

MORGANS
28 NE 29th St., Miami: 305-573-9678 / **Wynwood**
themorgansrestaurant.com
CUISINE: American
DRINKS: Full bar

SERVING: B'fast / Lunch / Dinner
They took an old Miami house built in the '30s and turned it into a restaurant. Food's always innovative and trendy. Weekend brunch.

NI.DO. CAFFÈ
7295 Biscayne Blvd., Miami: 305-960-7022 / **Biscayne Corridor**
http://www.nidocaffe.us
CUISINE: Italian
DRINKS: Beer/ Wine
SERVING: Lunch / Dinner
Mozzarella bar. They make it here. Artichoke soufflé, tuna tartare. Very comfy feeling here.

SALUMERIA104
3451 NE First Ave, Miami, 305-424-9588 / **Midtown**
www.salumeria104.com
CUISINE: Italian
DRINKS: Beer & Wine Only
SERVING: Brunch, Lunch & Dinner
PRICE RANGE: $$
Great place for an authentic Italian meal. Menu features a variety of Italian cured meats, pastas, and specials. Menu picks include: Beef lasagna and Antipasto. Nice approachable wine list.

SHOKUDO BY WORLD RESOURCE CAFE

4740 NE 2nd Ave., Miami: 305-758-7782 / **Design District**

www.shokudomiami.com

CUISINE: Asian Fusion

DRINKS: Beer & Wine

SERVING: Lunch, Dinner

Elegant but casual setting serving tasty dishes like Ahi Tuna Poke, SISIG - Sizzling Pork Cheek Buns and house-made dumplings. Impeccable service. $$

ST. ROCH MARKET

140 NE 39th St Suite #241, Miami, 786-542-8977

https://miami.strochmarket.com/

CUISINE: American (New)

DRINKS: Full bar

SERVING: Breakfast, Lunch, and Dinner

NEIGHBORHOOD: Design District

PRICE RANGE: $$-$$$

This gourmet food hall has an impressive selection of global fare. The design treatment behind the bar, with these scoops cut out of the framework, makes this place look like one of those bars in "Star Wars." But the atmosphere is quite different—all modern, sharp edges, comfortable and welcoming. You could eat lunch and dinner here every day for a week and not scratch the surface. And it would all be great fun. In the middle of the high-end shopping the Design District is known for. Some food halls offer a specialized focus: Italian at **Casa Tua Cicina**, Asian at **1-800-Lucky**, for example. Here you have a wide selection, and it's a great place to try samples of different cuisines. Southern food. Mexican food. Vegan. Italian, Tacos, Ceviche, Sushi, Peruvian, Israeli, Juices, Caribbean, Vietnamese, Asian. Craft cocktail bar. Outdoor seating. Pet friendly.

SUGARCANE RAW BAR GRILL

3252 NE 1st Ave., Miami: 786 369-0353 / **Midtown**
http://www.sugarcanerawbargrill.com
CUISINE: International
DRINKS: Full Bar
SERVING: Lunch/ Dinner
One of the hippest spots in Midtown. All kinds of things
going on with this menu, which ranges all over the world.
Great raw bar items. I find it very expensive. As if by
offering "small plates," they can charge you a lot of money
for a small portion. Still, the food is incredibly good with
creative twists and an unusual use of exotic ingredients
that will keep your head spinning. How about bacon-
wrapped dates? Sounds awful, right? It's not. A big fat
date is stuffed with Manchego cheese, linguiça sausage
and then wrapped in bacon. Way busy on weekends.
Indoor-outdoor. $$$$

WYNWOOD KITCHEN & BAR

2550 NW 2nd Ave., Miami: 305-772-8959 / **Wynwood**
www.wynwoodkitchenandbar.com
CUISINE: American
DRINKS: Beer/ Wine
SERVING: Lunch/ Dinner
Tony Goldman was one of the original New York
developers who came to South Beach and saw in the Art
Deco District what none of the local developers saw: a
gold mine. (When he died in 2012, he still owned the **Park
Central Hotel**, his flagship property on **Ocean Drive**.) He
never rested on his laurels. He was a big mover and shaker
in Wynwood, owning lots of property. What **Craig
Robins** wrought in the Design District, Tony Goldman has
wrought in Wynwood, to wit: put it on the map. This was
his restaurant, and you'll love it. (Son **Joey** owns the
eponymous Italian eatery a few feet away.) The way

they've decorated the walls with graffiti-style art will remind you why you're not a decorator: who would have thought of this? Food? Very much a bistro style menu, but with influences all over the place. I like the "clay pots," whole meals served in little pots. Choose from chicken curry, the snapper and mussel curry or the braised beef (my favorite of the three: short ribs, sweet soy, caramelized leeks, pickled chilies). Also a standout: the cod fish oreganata and the hanger steak frites. Satisfying sandwiches and salads as well. Don't forget to walk around the grounds outside to have a look at the graffiti art. $$$

DOWNTOWN-BRICKELL

There really is a lot going on Downtown. From the to the wizardry of Daniel Boulud at **db Bistro Moderne**, you'll find everything from high quality Indonesian food for $5 at **Bali Café** (no credit cards, cash only) to slices of sashimi at **Zuma** that will cost you twice that for one slice. But it takes some getting used to navigating your way around Downtown. It's congested, everything jammed together, annoying one-way streets, aggravating—and all very exciting. Best is to take someone who knows the area if you're rushed for time.

AREA 31
270 Biscayne Boulevard Way, Miami: 305-424-5234
www.area31restaurant.com
CUISINE: Seafood, Mediterranean
DRINKS: Full Bar
SERVING: B'fast / Lunch / Dinner
Hard to beat the environment they've created down here. From the vantage point of the 16th floor here at the Epic, you get a spectacular view of all the buildings downtown

(from inside or outside on their terrace). You feel like you're in a huge metropolis, surrounded by all these glamorous towers. This is NOT the Miami that you get down on street level.

Anyway, the food and drinks are just as spectacular as the view. (Bring your expense account privileges.) The "Area 31" in the name refers to what I presume some official body has determined is a sustainable fishing area that extends from the Carolinas down along the Florida coast, though this can't possibly be true. Still, it's a great marketing hook and you feel free to order anything you want.

Specialties are seafood prepared with a Mediterranean twist.

Lunch: try the pork belly sliders or the smoked turkey club.

Dinner: focus on the fish: yellowtail snapper, the shrimp ravioli are excellent.

What the chef does quite well is use unusual ingredients in all his dishes. His croquettas have tomato jam, diced plantains and cilantro along with the chorizo. His yellowfin tuna will come with radishes, pickled cucumber, quinoa and shoyu.

Here, you're in the hands of a master.

(One of those hands will be in your wallet!) $$$$

BALI CAFÉ
109 NE 2nd Ave., Miami: 305-358-5751
http://balicafe.food93.com/
CUISINE: Indonesia; sushi; Asian fusion
DRINKS: Beer/Wine
SERVING: Lunch / Dinner – **CASH ONLY**
This place is noted because it was written up in the Herald that low-wage Indonesian cruise ship workers who get like half a day off when their ships come in to pick up new

passengers head out in droves to this tiny place in Downtown.

Well, everybody else started coming here too. And since the underpaid cruise ship workers are only here once a week, you get the rest of the week to try it out. If you've never had this kind of food, get the *rijsttafel*, which is a kind of sampler. All good food. Cheap. $. CASH ONLY.

THE BAR AT LEVEL 25 (CONRAD HOTEL)
1395 Brickell Ave., Miami: 305-503-6500
www.conradmiami.com
CUISINE: Tapas
DRINKS: Full Bar
SERVING: Lunch / Dinner
They serve sandwiches at lunch and have a raw bar with creative tapas dishes in the evening. Another great view of Downtown. $$$$

BOULUD SUD MIAMI
JW Marriott Marquis, 255 Biscayne Blvd. Way, Miami: 305-421-8800
https://www.bouludsud.com/miami/
CUISINE: French, American
DRINKS: Full Bar
SERVING: Lunch / Dinner

Daniel Boulud's take on American food using Florida ingredients, with his French twist, of course. The result: spectacular. All in the stunning modern setting of this downtown hotel. Very luxe. His burger has gotten famous: a stack that includes *foie gras*, short ribs and black truffles. (Oh, and there's a burger stuffed in there too.) Bring a Lipitor. (Honestly, avoid the burger and focus on the fish.) $$$$

CAPITAL GRILLE
444 Brickell Ave., Miami: 305 374-4500
http://www.thecapitalgrille.com
CUISINE: Steakhouse
DRINKS: Full Bar
SERVING: Lunch weekdays/Dinner nightly
Dry-aged steaks and an award-winning wine list are the draw at this "power lunch" spot. Same sort of menu you already know about. Still, the lobster mac & cheese is a standout. $$$$

CASA TUA CUCINA
Brickell City Centre
70 SW 7th St, Miami, 305-755-0320
https://www.brickellcitycentre.com/
CUISINE: Italian/Mediterranean
DRINKS: Full bar
SERVING: Breakfast, Lunch, and Dinner
NEIGHBORHOOD: Downtown
PRICE RANGE: $$-$$$
Upscale food hall featuring a huge variety of Italian fare – everything from pasta, pizza, salads, and pastries. The space was carved out of the Saks Fifth Avenue store. Each of less than a dozen stalls features a different Italian specialty. You order from a stall, grab a table and a waiter will bring your order, finding you by your number. A wine bar serves all the stalls. Food is really good. Vegan

options. Brunch menu in the mornings. Coffee and crafted cocktails. Free Wi-Fi.

CIPRIANI
465 Brickell Ave., Miami, 786-329-4090
www.cipriani.com
CUISINE: Italian
DRINKS: Full Bar
SERVING: Lunch-Dinner daily
PRICE RANGE: $$$$
NEIGHBORHOOD: Brickell
The Cipriani family has made good use of its legendary history, parlaying it into a chain of upmarket restaurants around the world. But they've come a long way since Ernest Hemingway drank in the modest Harry's Bar in Venice. A long way indeed. Ignazio Cipriani is great grandson to Giuseppe, who opened Harry's in 1931. There are 2 levels to this location, and they seat a whopping 400, so it's a massive undertaking. Floor-to-ceiling windows look out onto panoramic views of the Bay. White leather seats and walnut paneling add to the look. The service is professional, but the two times I've been, the waiters were bossy to the point of rudeness. There's way too much steering you to this dish or that wine. Italian specialties are good, but plan on a LONG lunch or dinner. They're in no rush and you better not be.

CRAZY ABOUT YOU
1155 Brickell Bay Dr. #101, Miami: 305-377-4442
www.crazyaboutyourestaurant.com
CUISINE: Mediterranean, Italian, Spanish
DRINKS: Full Bar
SERVING: Lunch / Dinner
Great views. Widely varied menu: chihuahua cheese appetizer; lentil soup, spinach salad; half roasted chicken;

red pepper hummus; slow braised steak with creamy arborio rice.

CRUST
668 NW 5TH St., Miami, 305-371-7065
www.**crust**-usa.com
CUISINE: Pizza / Mediterranean
DRINKS: Beer & Wine Only
SERVING: Dinner; closed Mondays
PRICE RANGE: $$
Chef Klime Kovaceski's Italian eatery specializes in pizza with gourmet toppings like figs, pesto-artichoke and fresh basil. The creative menu offers a variety of Mediterranean dishes from chef Kovaceski's personal recipes. Delivery available.

DOLORES, BUT YOU CAN CALL ME LOLITA
1000 S. Miami Ave., Miami: 305-403-3103
www.doloreslolita.com
CUISINE: American
DRINKS: Full Bar
SERVING: Lunch / Dinner
Romantic setting (except when it's jammed on weekend nights). Try to get a table on the patio upstairs. Pappardelle with kobe beef Bolognese; filet mignon funghi. $$$

EDGE STEAK & BAR
Four Seasons Hotel, 1435 Brickell Ave, Miami, 305-381-3190
www.edgerestaurantmiami.com
CUISINE: Seafood/Steakhouse/American (New)
DRINKS: Full bar
SERVING: Dinner
PRICE RANGE: $$$
NEIGHBORHOOD: Brickell

Luxury steakhouse located in the Four Season Hotel so expect the best. Located on the 7th floor of the Four Season, this eatery offers a great dining experience. Menu picks include: Pork & Pistachio Terrine and Chicken Liver and Foie Gras Pâté. Great choice for brunch.

FOOQ'S
1035 N Miami Ave, Miami, 786-536-2749
www.fooqsmiami.com
CUISINE: Persian / American (New)
DRINKS: Beer & Wine Only
SERVING: Dinner Tues-Sun; Lunch on Sun; Closed Mon
PRICE RANGE: $$$
NEIGHBORHOOD: **Downtown**
Located in downtown Miami's "nightclub" district, this unique eatery offers American fare with a Persian twist. Favorites: Braised lamb; Khoresh (which is Persian stew) and Delmonico steak. Reservations recommended.

FRATELLI MILANO
213 SE 1st St., Miami: 305-373-2300
www.ristorantefratellimilano.com
CUISINE: Italian
DRINKS: Beer/Wine
SERVING: Lunch / Dinner; closed Sunday.
Bucatini san Babila, thick pasta with sweet Italian sausage, broccoli, garlic, pecorino cheese in a tomato sauce; Fettuccine Allo Scoglio, homemade fettuccine, sauteed shrimp, scallops, calamari and mussels in a white wine sauce; lobster ravioli; Fiocchi di Pera.
$$-$$$

GARCIA'S SEAFOOD GRILLE & FISH MARKET
398 NW N. River Dr., Miami: 305-375-0765
www.garciasseafoodgrill.com
CUISINE: Seafood

DRINKS: Full Bar
SERVING: Lunch / Dinner
Long a popular seafood eatery on the Miami River. Just concentrate on the seafood, seafood, seafood. During stone crab season, they usually have a 2-4-1 special on Friday. A friend of mine with a boat goes down almost every Friday during season to get them, tying up at the dock in front of this place. Makes for a great afternoon. (I'm not listing **Casablanca,** which is just next door, but, many people prefer it over Garcia's. Me? I can't really tell the difference. They're both excellent.) $$-$$$

GRAZIANO'S RESTAURANT BRICKELL
177 SW 7th St., Miami: 305 860-1426
http://www.grazianosgroup.com
CUISINE: Argentine
DRINKS: full bar
SERVING: B'fast / Lunch / Dinner
Argentine steak house. Top quality meats, as would be expected. There's a great bakery here, so you have to go through it to the restaurant behind. Pastas with chicken is good if you're not into meats. There are chips with truffle oil dribbled over them. Also the spinach gnocchi. They have an excellent selection of Malbecs here – ask them to suggest a reasonably priced one (don't let them give you one for more than $35) if you're not familiar with this rich, red Argentine wine. $$$

HARD ROCK CAFE
Bayside Marketplace
401 Biscayne Blvd., Miami: 305 377-3110
http://www.hardrock.com
CUISINE: American
DRINKS: Full Bar
SERVING: Lunch / Dinner

You know what to expect here. Nothing too different. Standard chain menu. Nice overlooking marina at Bayside. Indoor-outdoor. $$$

II GABBIANO
335 S. Biscayne Blvd., Miami: 305-373-0063
www.ilgabbianomia.com
CUISINE: Italian
DRINKS: Full Bar
SERVING: Lunch weekdays, noon to 3; dinner from 5; closed Sunday.
Where the Miami River meets the Bay, you'll find this super excellent Italian restaurant. Everything you've heard about it is true: it may be the best Italian restaurant in all of Florida, one of the best in the country. (**Scarpetta** in the **Fontainebleau** is right up there with this.) Fried zucchini, gnocchi with gorgonzola, mushroom ravioli ($39), grilled calamari is excellent; alla Scarpariello; spaghetti alla carbonara; ricotta cheesecake. Whatever pennies you have, this place is worth the last one. $$$$$

KIKI ON THE RIVER
450 NW North River Dr, Miami, 786-502-3243
www.kikiontheriver.com
CUISINE: Greek/Mediterranean
DRINKS: Beer & Wine Only
SERVING: Full Bar
PRICE RANGE: $$$$
NEIGHBORHOOD: Downtown
Chic waterfront eatery on the Miami River offers a menu of traditional Greek cuisine and seafood. It's a big spot that they spent a fortune on, with wooden planks outside facing the river, where you can dock a boat if you have one. It's hot in the summer, even with the fans whirring all around you. There is an indoor dining room, but it's no fun compared to outside. Favorites: Grilled octopus and

Grilled scallops. Great cocktails. Can get crowded on the weekends and when they turn up the music, it's hard to bear. (Tip: save a fortune by coming during the week for lunch when they have a very reasonably priced prix fixe.)

KOMODO
801 Brickell Ave, Miami, 305-534-2211
www.komodomiami.com
CUISINE: Chinese/Asian Fusion
DRINKS: Full bar
SERVING: Lunch/Dinner; Dinner only on Sat & Sun
PRICE RANGE: $$$$
NEIGHBORHOOD: Brickell
Upscale eatery offering a high-end menu of Southeastern Asian fare. Massive multi-level dining room with dining indoors and out. Family-style menu items include favorites like: Lobster Dynamite and Grilled Szechuan Beef.

LA LOGGIA RISTORANTE AND LOUNGE
68 W. Flagler St., Miami: 305-373-4800
www.laloggiamiami.com
WEBSITE DOWN AT PRESSTIME
CUISINE: Italian
DRINKS: Full Bar
SERVING: Lunch / Dinner
Inexpensive, family style Italian food. $$$

LA MOON
97 SW 8th St., Miami: 305-860-6209
No Website
CUISINE: Colombian
DRINKS: Beer/Wine
SERVING: Lunch / Dinner/Late night
Excellent quality cheap Colombian food. $

LARGO BAR & GRILL
Bayside, 401 Biscayne Blvd., Miami 305-374-9706
www.largobarandgrill.com
WEBSITE DOWN AT PRESSTIME
CUISINE: American
DRINKS: Full Bar
SERVING: Lunch / Dinner
Avoid Hooters and the Hard Rock and opt for this if
you're in the downtown "tourist trap" called Bayside.
Buffalo chicken salad, Philly cheesesteak, Angus sliders,
crab cake sandwich, seafood Alfredo, chicken parm,
scampi over pasta. $$-$$$

LOS GAUCHITOS STEAKHOUSE
The Doubletree Grand
1717 N. Bayshore Dr., Miami: 305-377-3133
www.biscaynebay.doubletree.com
CUISINE: Argentine steakhouse
DRINKS: Full Bar
SERVING: Lunch / Dinner
It's OK, but if this is the kind of food you want, there are
many other better places similarly priced. Keep reading.
$$$

NAOE
661Brickell Key Dr, Miami, 305-947-6263
www.naoemiami.com
CUISINE: Seafood/Steakhouse/Live Raw Food
DRINKS: Beer & Wine Only
SERVING: Dinner
PRICE RANGE: $$$$
NEIGHBORHOOD: Brickell

Contemporary Japanese bistro offering a creative fixed-price (Omakase) menu. Note there's no sign on the front door so you must look for the number 661. Definitely a culinary experience for fans of sushi and the chef offers seconds of any piece of sushi served during your meal. Not for the budget diners. Reservations recommended.

NOVECENTO
1414 Brickell Ave.,Miami: 305-403-0900
www.novecento.com
CUISINE: Contemporary Argentine
DRINKS: Full Bar
SERVING: Lunch / Dinner
Not just steaks; excellent seafood as well. $$-$$$

NOVIKOV
300 S Biscayne Blvd, Miami, 305-489-1000
https://www.novikovmiami.com/
CUISINE: Chinese/Japanese/Seafood
DRINKS: Full bar
SERVING: Lunch and Dinner, Dinner only on Sat.
NEIGHBORHOOD: Downtown

PRICE RANGE: $$$$
Upscale world-renowned eatery (with outposts in London, Dubai, Tokyo) featuring a globally sourced menu of robata grill and wok dishes. The interior is sleek, modern, refreshing. Great display of fish on ice from all over the world. Extensive Dim Sum and Sushi selection. Favorites: Grilled Branzino scallion & ginger; Peking Duck is a specialty; Wagyu skirt steak and Salmon maki. (The corn on the cob side is excellent.) Vegan options. Delicious desserts. Outdoor seating.

PEGA GRILL
15 E. Flagler St., Miami: 305-808-6666
www.pegagrill.com
CUISINE: Greek
DRINKS: Beer/Wine
SERVING: Lunch
Nice spot for good Greek food that's fast and cheap. $$

RIVER OYSTER BAR
also known as **RIVER SEAFOOD & OYSTER BAR**
650 S. Miami Ave., Miami: 305-530-1915
www.therivermiami.com
CUISINE: Seafood
DRINKS: Full Bar
SERVING: Lunch / Dinner
Though they have a substantial menu, I don't think I've sat at a table here in years. I always slither up to the bar and order a couple of dozen oysters mixed from the selection they currently have available. And have a bottle of wine or a couple of beers. $$$

RIVERWALK CAFE
Hyatt Regency Miami
400 SE 2nd Ave., Miami: 305 358-1234

www.hyatt.com/en-US/hotel/florida/hyatt-regency-miami/miarm/dining
CUISINE: American; some Latin
DRINKS: Full Bar
SERVING: B'fast / Lunch / Dinner
Typical hotel restaurant offering the expected American menu with a few "Latin" items thrown in to remind you that you're in Miami. Better than eating here, go outside and get the real thing. $$$

SOYA & POMODORO
120 NE 1st St., Miami: 305-381-9511
www.soyaepomodoro.com
CUISINE: Italian
DRINKS: Beer/Wine
SERVING: Lunch (weekdays); Dinner (Thursday-Saturday)
This charming little spot is located in the old Dupont Building, so you're immediately enclosed in an architectural style that will make you feel like you're in Europe. Food is good, cheap Italian, from the south. $-$$

SPARKY'S ROADSIDE RESTAURANT & BAR
204 NE 1st St., Miami: 305-377-2877
www.sparkysroadsidebarbecue.com
CUISINE: Barbeque
DRINKS: Beer/Wine
SERVING: Lunch / Dinner
BBQ in the dry-rubbed style. Very nice. They make their
own sauces. $-$$

SUVICHE
49 SW 11th St., Miami: 305-960-7097
www.suviche.com
CUISINE: Sushi, Peruvian, Japanese
DRINKS: Beer/Wine
SERVING: Lunch / Dinner
Tiny, tiny place serving excellent Peruvian-Japanese food.
$$

TORO TORO
Intercontinental
100 Chopin Plaza, Miami: 305-372-4710
www.torotoromiami.com
CUISINE: Latin American, Steakhouse, Tapas
DRINKS: Full Bar
SERVING: Lunch, Dinner
Authentic Latin American dishes in Miami's iconic
InterContinental Hotel. Delicious menu items include
dozens of tapas, flat bread pizza, and lamb anticuchos.
Also grouper pan-roasted and a caldo de pollo. For lunch,
get the pepito steak sandwich. $$$

TRULUCK'S SEAFOOD, STEAK & CRABHOUSE
777 Brickell Ave., Miami: 305-579-0035
www.trulucks.com
CUISINE: Seafood, Steakhouse

DRINKS: Full Bar
SERVING: Lunch (weekdays) /Dinner nightly
Most steakhouses offer big lobsters just because they can,
but their hearts are with the steaks. Here, it's just the
opposite. While you can get really great steaks, their hearts
are with the seafood. (They catch their own stone crabs,
and it's cheaper than Joe's). Fine menu complemented by
very good service. $$$-$$$$

WOLFGANG'S STEAKHOUSE
315 S Biscayne Blvd., Miami, 305-487-7130
http://wolfgangssteakhouse.net/miami/
CUISINE: American; steakhouse
DRINKS: Full Bar
SERVING: Lunch-Dinner
PRICE RANGE: $$$$
NEIGHBORHOOD: Brickell
How many steakhouses can Miami absorb? If we had to
have another one, at least we got a good one with
Wolfgang's. The Porterhouse for 2
is a marvel of texture and flavor. They have lobster and
sea bass on the menu, but stick to the steaks. Wolfgang
Zwiener was head waiter at the legendary Peter Luger's in
Brooklyn before leaving to open his flagship

location on Park Avenue. Miami is a better place because he came here, too. In fact, I think it's way better than Peter Luger. Oh, and here you can use a credit card, useless at Luger's, which even after all these years, still only take Cash.

ZEST
200 S Biscayne Blvd, Miami, 305-374-9378
www.zestmiami.com
CUISINE: American (New)/Caribbean
DRINKS: Full bar
SERVING: Lunch & Dinner; Dinner only on Sat; closed Sun
PRICE RANGE: $$
NEIGHBORHOOD: Downtown
Modern eatery with a menu of creative island fare from Chef Cindy Hutson. Menu favorites include: Ceviche, Yellowtail snapper, and Cornish hen. Regulars rave about the salmon coated with coffee and cocoa. Save room for the amazing bread pudding.

ZUMA
Epic Hotel
270 Biscayne Blvd. Way, Miami: 305 577-0277
http://www.zumarestaurant.com
CUISINE: Japanese
DRINKS: Full Bar
SERVING: Lunch (till 3); dinner from 6.
This rave-inducing spot will thrill you if you're into Japanese fine food. Lobster tempura, ribeye with wafu sauce, salmon teriyaki, grilled scallops, black cod, mushroom risotto. You'll love the view overlooking the docks and the River. $$$$

LITTLE HAVAVA

While there's a lot more to Little Havana than Cuban food, it's the Cuban food you come for.

ANTIGUA GUATEMALA CAFETERIA
2741 W Flagler St., Miami: 305-643-0304
No web site
CUISINE: Central American
DRINKS: Beer/ Wine
SERVING: B'fast / Lunch / Dinner
Although the name suggests differently, this eatery serves up mostly Central American dishes. Pupusas (corn tortillas stuffed with cheese, beans, chicharron, or a revuelto, a combination of all three), a variety of daily soups, stuffed peppers, pickled pork and churrasco. $

CASA JUANCHO
2436 SW 8th St., Miami: 305-642-2524
http://www.casajuancho.com
CUISINE: Spanish
DRINKS: Full Bar
SERVING: Lunch / Dinner
In this well-known eatery, Spanish delicacies include baby eel and hand carved ham from acorn fed Iberian pigs. $$$$

DON CAMARON SEAFOOD GRILL
501 NW 37 Ave., Miami: 305-642-6767
www.doncamaronrestaurant.com
CUISINE: Seafood
DRINKS: Beer/ Wine
SERVING: B'fast / Lunch / Dinner
Here you will find everything seafood; fish dishes come with rice and your choice of plantains or French fries. Get there early; this place fills up fast. $-$$

EL JACALITO TAQUERIA MEXICANA
3622 W Flagler St., Miami: 305-443-1336
www.jacalitomexicanrestaurant.com
CUISINE: Mexican
DRINKS: Beer/ Wine
SERVING: B'fast / Lunch / Dinner
You will feel right at home in this small and quaint
restaurant. Although they serve up traditional Mexican
dishes, it's the tacos that are a must have. Huge selection
of tacos including tongue, cow cheek, cochinita pibil
(shredded pork), chorizo, beef, chicken, and vegetables. $-
$$

EL PALACIO DE LOS JUGOS
5721 W Flagler St., Miami: 305-264-1503
www.elpalaciodelosjugos.com
SEVERAL LOCATIONS
CUISINE: Cuban

DRINKS: No Alcohol
SERVING: B'fast / Lunch / Dinner
This landmark is a one-stop shop including a market overflowing with fresh fruits and vegetables and a juice bar serving an array of juices and *batidos*. But their cafeteria style prepared foods you can get here is **some of the best Cuban food you can get in Miami,** not the usual Cuban greasy slop you find on most corners. $

LA CAMARONERA FISH MARKET
1952 W. Flagler St., Miami: 305-642-3322
http://garciabrothersseafood.com
CUISINE: Cuban Seafood
DRINKS: No Alcohol
SERVING: B'fast / Lunch / Dinner
No seats in this eatery, just a counter that you can lean on making this place a true Cuban fish-fry. Get there early, it fills up fast. $

LA CARRETA
3632 SW 8th St., Miami: 305-444-7501
http://www.lacarreta.com
CUISINE: Cuban
DRINKS: Full Bar
SERVING: B'fast / Lunch / Dinner
Although not the most gourmet of Cuban cuisine, it is a great place to get traditional dishes. Great daily specials. $$

LA CASITA CUBAN CUISINE
3805 SW 8th St., Miami: 305-448-8224
www.lasvegascubancuisine.com
CUISINE: Cuban
DRINKS: Full Bar
SERVING: Lunch / Dinner

Surprisingly low-key and mellow, this place serves up delicious typical Cuban dishes at affordable prices. $

LAS TAPAS DE ROSA
449 SW 8th St., Miami: 305-856-9788
www.tapasderosa.com
CUISINE: Spanish, Tapas
DRINKS: Beer & Wine
SERVING: Lunch, Dinner
This little family-run restaurant is known for serving some of the best tapas in Miami, almost all under $10. Old World feel, friendly service, and extensive Spanish wine list. $$

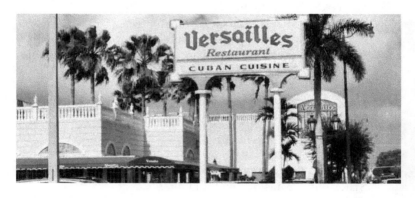

VERSAILLES
3555 SW 8th St., Miami: 305-444-0240
www.versaillesrestaurant.com
CUISINE: Cuban
DRINKS: Full Bar
SERVING: B'fast / Lunch / Dinner
A staple of the Cuban community, this is as authentic as it gets. Every politician, from mayor to president, comes by this place to woo the Cuban vote & drum up support. But I've never thought the food was *that* good. I've had much

better Cuban food a dozen other places. The Cuban coffee is a must have, of course. $$

CORAL GABLES

Coral Gables has never been known for excitement. In fact, the city fathers are so aware of the city's image that they seek to control just about everything, from the size of a realtor's sign on a lawn to the color of a newspaper box on the corner.

But as dull as the Gables can be, one place where the excitement has always been at the uppermost level is in the field of fine dining.

Even with the explosion of great restaurants on South Beach (and more lately, Downtown), the swank eateries in the Gables have held their own, and make the "City Beautiful" really a "City Bountiful."

BRASSERIE CENTRAL
320 San Lorenzo Ave, Coral Gables, 786-536-9388
www.brasseriecentralmiami.com
CUISINE: French
DRINKS: Full Bar
SERVING: Dinner
PRICE RANGE: $$
NEIGHBORHOOD: Merrick Park/Coral Gables
Cute brasserie serving classic French fare with the atmosphere of a Parisian café. Menu picks: Saumon Fume Ecossais (smoked Salmon) and fresh Pate. Raw bar. Nice selection of wines and champagne.

BULLA GASTROBAR
2500 Ponce De Leon Blvd, Coral Gables, 786-509-7751
https://bullagastrobar.com/locations/coral-gables/

CUISINE: Spanish/Tapas Bar
DRINKS: Full Bar
SERVING: Lunch & Dinner
PRICE RANGE: $$
NEIGHBORHOOD: Coral Gables
Popular eatery serving Spanish and Catalan dishes.
Favorites: Patatas Bravas and Huevos Bulla. Variety of
tapas (more than 20) and daily specials.

CAFFE ABBRACCI
318 Aragon Ave., Coral Gables: 305-441-0700
http://www.caffeabbracci.com
CUSINE: Italian
DRINKS: Full Bar
SERVING: Lunch / Dinner
True to his native Venezia, owner Nino Pernetti continues
his time-honored tradition of bringing quintessential
classic Northern Italian dishes to his customers in this
"power" lunch and dinner spot. A lot of big shots eat here,
but Nino makes them pay for the privilege. Indoor-
outdoor. $$$$

CANTON AND SUSHI MAKI
2614 Ponce de Leon Blvd., Coral Gables: 305-448-3736
http://www.cantonrestaurants.com
CUSINE: Sushi
DRINKS: Beer/Wine
SERVING: Lunch / Dinner
Good Chinese and sushi since 1975, specializing in
generously portioned Chinese cuisine served family style
for dine-in, take-out, delivery and catering. $$

CHRISTY'S
3101 Ponce de Leon Blvd., Coral Gables: 305-446-1400
http://www.christysrestaurant.com
CUSINE: Steakhouse

DRINKS: Full Bar
SERVING: Dinner
Diners at this Miami landmark restaurant enjoy the famous
Caesar salad, aged Midwestern beef and the daily fresh
Florida seafood. Impossible to go wrong here. $$$$

EATING HOUSE
Located in Cafe Ponce
804 Ponce De Leon Blvd, Coral Gables, 305-448-6524
www.eatinghousemiami.com
CUISINE: American (New)
DRINKS: Beer & Wine
SERVING: Lunch & Dinner, Lunch only on Sat; closed
Mondays
PRICE RANGE: $$
NEIGHBORHOOD:
Small eatery serving a menu of locally sourced dishes.
Menu picks: Pasta carbonara and Chicken & waffles.
Usually busy with a wait. Reservations recommended.

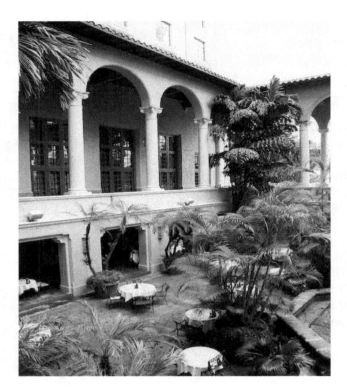

FONTANA
The Biltmore
1200 Anastasia Ave., Coral Gables: 305-913-3200
http://www.biltmorehotel.com
CUSINE: Mediterranean
DRINKS: Full Bar
SERVING: B'fast / Lunch / Dinner
Enjoy authentic Italian cuisine in a casual brasserie featuring outdoor dining in a courtyard setting. Main reason to come here is to see the famous hotel. $$$$

FRATELLINO
264 Miracle Mile, Coral Gables, 786-452-0068
No Website

CUISINE: Italian
DRINKS: Beer & Wine Only
SERVING: Lunch/Dinner; Dinner-only on Sun
PRICE RANGE: $$
NEIGHBORHOOD: Coral Gables
Small intimate eatery offering delicious Italian fare. Menu picks include: Risotto alla Pescatora and Risotto alla Pescatora. Also a big favorite is the fried calamari & zucchini. Delicious tiramisu and cheesecake.

FRENCHIE'S DINER
2618 Galiano St, Coral Gables, 305-442-4554
www.frenchiesdiner.com
CUISINE: French
DRINKS: Beer & Wine
SERVING: Lunch & Dinner; closed Sun & Mon
PRICE RANGE: $$
NEIGHBORHOOD: Coral Gables
Friendly eatery offering typical diner fare along with creative daily specials. Favorites: Duck Club Sandwich and Risotto with wild mushrooms.

GRAZIANO'S
394 Giralda Ave., Coral Gables: 305-774 3599
http://www.grazianosgroup.com
CUSINE: Argentine Steakhouse
DRINKS: Full Bar
SERVING: Lunch / Dinner
This restaurant is a traditional Argentinean steakhouse. A nice experience for meat and wine lovers. Also pastas, salads and seafood. $$$

HILLSTONE RESTAURANT
201 Miracle Mile, Coral Gables, 305-529-0141
www.hillstone.com
CUISINE: American (New)/Sushi

DRINKS: Full bar
SERVING: Lunch/Dinner
PRICE RANGE: $$$
NEIGHBORHOOD: Coral Gables
Upscale restaurant offering a menu of steak, sushi, seafood, and pastas.
Upscale chain eatery featuring steak, seafood & pasta alongside specialty cocktails. Great meat sandwiches and amazing salads. Try their signature dessert tres leches with fresh fruit. Nice wine selection. Reservations a must on weekends.

LA PALMA RISTORANTE
116 Alhambra Circle, Coral Gables: 305 445-8777
http://www.lapalmaristorante.com
CUSINE: Italian
DRINKS: Full Bar
SERVING: Lunch / Dinner
Northern Italian cuisine. Located in a restored historic building. Tree-covered courtyard with its stone fountain is both relaxing and romantic. The inside dining room's fine art gives guests the feeling of dining in a gallery. Outdoor dining. $$$$

LIBERTY CAFFE
997 N. Greenway Drive, Coral Gables: 305-392-1211
http://www.libertycaffe.com
CUSINE: Italian
DRINKS: Beer/Wine
SERVING: B'fast / Lunch / Dinner
This is the ideal neighborhood spot for a morning coffee or a cool gelato on a warm afternoon. House-made gelatos, pressed sandwiches, oven-baked pizza breads, specialty coffees and espresso. $$

MESAMAR
264 Giralda Ave, Coral Gables, 305-640-8448
www.mesamar.com
CUISINE: Seafood
DRINKS: Full bar
SERVING: Lunch & Dinner
PRICE RANGE: $$$$
MesaMar serves delicious seafood fusion with an Oriental influence. Favorites include: Tuna & lobster tacos and Calamari.

MORTON'S THE STEAKHOUSE
2333 Ponce De Leon Blvd., Coral Gables: 305 442-1662
http://www.mortons.com/coralgables
CUSINE: Steakhouse
DRINKS: Full Bar
SERVING: Lunch / Dinner
For more than 30 years this restaurant has served the finest quality food, featuring USDA prime-aged beef, fresh fish and seafood, big salads, delicious appetizers and elegant desserts. Indoor-outdoor. $$$$

ORTANIQUE ON THE MILE
278 Miracle Mile, Coral Gables: 305-446-7710
http://www.cindyhutsoncuisine.com
CUSINE: Caribbean
DRINKS: Full Bar
SERVING: Dinner
Fusion of American, Caribbean, Latin and Asian cuisine, served in a colorful tropical ambience. Great for people-watching on the Mile. $$$

PASCAL'S ON PONCE
2611 Ponce De Leon Blvd, Coral Gables, 305-444-2024
www.pascalmiami.com
CUISINE: French

DRINKS: Full Bar
SERVING: Lunch & Dinner, Dinner only on Sat; closed on Sundays
PRICE RANGE: $$$$
NEIGHBORHOOD: Coral Gables
Cozy bistro serving modern French fare. Favorites: Scallops and Crab cakes. Nice dessert selection. Impressive wine selection. Upscale dining experience.

RED FISH GRILL
9610 Old Cutler Road, Miami: 305- 668-8788
http://www.redfishgrill.net
CUSINE: Seafood
DRINKS: Beer/Wine
SERVING: Dinner
Located on the shore of Biscayne Bay in Matheson Hammock Park, this restaurant is a breath of fresh air at the water's edge. Get the pan-fried snapper ($30). The main treat here is the "old Florida" setting. Indoor-outdoor. $$$

RED KOI THAI & SUSHI LOUNGE

317 Miracle Mile, Coral Gables: 305- 446-2690
http://www.redkoilounge.com
CUSINE: Sushi/Thai
DRINKS: Full Bar
SERVING: Dinner
Asian fusion. Indoor-outdoor. $$$

RINCON ARGENTINO

2345 SW 37th Ave., Coral Gables: 305- 444-2494
http://www.rinconargentino.com
CUSINE: Latin/American
DRINKS: Full Bar
SERVING: Lunch / Dinner
Fine meats and homemade pastas in this Argentine eatery.
$$$

SAWA

Village of Merrick Park
360 San Lorenzo Ave., Coral Gables: 305-447-6555
http://www.sawarestaurant.com
CUSINE: Mediterranean
DRINKS: Full Bar
SERVING: Lunch / Dinner
Mediterranean and Japanese cuisines. (Huh?) Chef
Jouvens Jean merges an innovative sushi menu with a
memorable ensemble of tapas and entrees. Inside there are
white walls, white chandeliers, white leather upholstery,
vividly colorful interactive 3D artworks by Chady Elias,
and an LED light show behind the bar. On the patio, there
are billowing white curtains and white leather sofas, where
guests can puff away on flavored Hookahs. (Well…) $$$$

SEASONS 52

321 Miracle Mile, Coral Gables: 305- 442-8552
http://www.seasons52.com

CUSINE: American
DRINKS: Full Bar
SERVING: Lunch / Dinner
Comfy grill and wine bar always seems to have a
youngish, attractive crowd and the bar scene is fun, too.
They emphasize fresh ingredients. (The flatbreads here can
feed two, and they're cheap, cheap, cheap!) $$-$$$

SHULA'S 347 GRILL
6915 Red Road, Coral Gables: 305- 665-9661
shulas347gables.com
CUSINE: American
DRINKS: Full Bar
SERVING: Lunch / Dinner
This restaurant is named in honor of Hall of Fame football
coach Don Shula. It follows a long line of successful
restaurants, all founded on the same famous tradition of
Shula's Steak Houses. Indoor, outdoor. Lotsa fun, really.
$$$$

SPRING CHICKEN
1514 South Dixie Hwy, Coral Gables, 305-699-6098
www.eatspringchicken.com
CUISINE: Southern/Traditional American
DRINKS: Full bar
SERVING: Lunch & Dinner
PRICE RANGE: $$$
NEIGHBORHOOD: Coral Gables
Bright and airy restaurant with simple décor and down-
home atmosphere. They stand by their motto: Live well.
Eat Well. Love every Bite. Here you'll find a menu of
classic southern fare like southern fried chicken with
biscuits. Like sister eatery Yardbird, the customers leave
satisfied.

THREEFOLD CAFÉ

141 Giralda Ave, Coral Gables, 305-704-8007
www.threefoldcafe.com
CUISINE: Australian/Cafe
DRINKS: Full bar
SERVING: Breakfast & Lunch; Dinner on Thur, Fri & Sat
PRICE RANGE: $$
NEIGHBORHOOD: Downtown
Great choice for a gourmet breakfast or brunch serving top
notch coffee and creative breakfast treats. Delicious
breads, benedicts, and French toast. Fresh juices and
homemade breads.

TWO SISTERS RESTAURANT

Hyatt Regency
50 Alhambra Plaza, Coral Gables: 305- 441-1234
https://coralgables.regency.hyatt.com/en/hotel/dining/Two
SistersRestaurant.html
CUSINE: French/Greek/Mediterranean
DRINKS: Full Bar
SERVING: B'fast / Lunch / Dinner
With the wide variety of things going on with this menu,
they should have named it **Four Sisters Who Can't Make
Up Their Mind!** $$$

XIXON SPANISH RESTAURANT

2101 Coral Way, Miami, 305-854-9350
www.xixonspanishrestaurant.com
CUISINE: Spanish/Tapas Bar
DRINKS: Full Bar
SERVING: Lunch & Dinner
PRICE RANGE: $$
NEIGHBORHOOD: Shenandoah
This modern multi-level Spanish eatery featuring several
rooms—a dining room, wine cellar and bakery/deli—is
one of my favorite spots in the Gables. The bakery/deli &

market give it a bustling feel most restaurants would die for. Food is uniformly outstanding. Large menu. Favorites: Seafood paella and Manchego. Lots of great dishes to share like fried artichokes and octopus. They get the cod from the chilly waters off Iceland.

COCONUT GROVE

While the days of Coconut Grove's ascendency in Miami is just a faded memory, there still are a few restaurants nice enough to warrant a visit.

ARIETE
3540 Main Hwy, Coconut Grove, 305-640-5862
www.arietemiami.com
CUISINE: American (New)
DRINKS: Full Bar
SERVING: Dinner Tues – Sun, Lunch Sat & Sun; closed Monday
PRICE RANGE: $$$
NEIGHBORHOOD: Coconut Grove
Modern farmhouse décor (snugly arranged wooden tables) with a bar on one side of the room and an open kitchen and a wood-burning oven on the other with an ever-changing menu of American fare. Favorites: Grilled oysters, Short rib and Venison. The small plates are really small. (Too small.) By way of contrast, the Painted Hills rib eye fills the whole plate and can feed 3. Great place for weekend brunch (if you don't mind spotty service). Classic cocktails. Music tends to be intrusively loud.

CHUG'S
3444 Main Hwy Suite 21, Coconut Grove, 786-534-8722
www.chugsdiner.com
CUISINE: Cuban Diner

DRINKS: Beer & Wine
SERVING: Breakfast, Lunch, and Dinner
PRICE RANGE: $
Authentic Cuban eatery serving favorites like Short Rib
Croquets, Pan con Lechon and of course Café con leche.
Plenty of outdoor seating. Wow! Someplace cheap to eat
in the Grove.

EL CARAJO
2465 SW 17th Ave., Miami: 305 856-2424
http://www.el-carajo.com
CUISINE: Spanish; tapas.
DRINKS: beer/wine.
SERVING: lunch, dinner daily.
Huge wine selection (1500 in stock). Small place, seats
only 55, but good, solid food. $-$$.

GLASS AND VINE
2820 McFarlane Rd, Coconut Grove, 305-200-5268
www.glassandvine.com
CUISINE: American (New)
DRINKS: Full Bar
SERVING: Lunch & Dinner
PRICE RANGE: $$
NEIGHBORHOOD: Coconut Grove
Located within Peacock Park, this indoor/outdoor eatery
offers an impressive Euro-style menu.
Favorites: Watermelon salad, Skewered broccoli and
Scallops, roasted lamb ribs. I'm a big fan of the iceberg
wedge. But here, they take whole baby heads of Romaine
and grill them with charred tomato, bacon, buttermilk and
blue cheese—little bits of buckwheat replace traditional
croutons. Outstanding! Intimate garden offers a great
dining experience.

JAGUAR CEVICHE SPOON BAR & LATAM GRILL
3067 Grand Ave, Coconut Grove: 305 444-0216
www.jaguarhg.com/restaurants
CUISINE: Latin.
DRINKS: full bar.
SERVING: lunch, dinner daily.
Ceviches served in large white ceramic spoons. Try
something different: *chiles en nogada*, which is a dish
made with poblano peppers jammed with pork and
covered in a walnut-cream sauce. The Latam Grill has
grilled steaks and seafood. All very nice. The meats are
paired with distinctive Latin salsas. Indoor, outdoor.
Casual. $$$-$$$$

LOCAL
3190 Commodore Plaza, Miami, 305-442-3377
www.lokalmiami.com
CUISINE: Burgers/American (New)
DRINKS: Beer & Wine
SERVING: Lunch and Dinner
PRICE RANGE: $$
Casual laid-back eatery offering a menu of burgers,
sandwiches and beer. (Menu items are made with local,
sustainable ingredients.) It's a little nicer than a dive,
which it would have to be in this location in the heart of
the Grove. You have to sell a lot of craft beer to pay the
rents on this street. Favorites: Steak Sandwich and "My
Childhood Dream" burger (their specialty).

LULU
3105 Commodore Plaza, Coconut Grove: 305 447-5858
http://www.luluinthegrove.com
CUISINE: Hard to pin down.
DRINKS: full bar.
SERVING: lunch, dinner daily.

Although the menu is all over the place, it's basically an American menu with a few things (like churrasco and some pastas) thrown in to give it some variety. Nice, cozy spot right in the heart of the Grove. $$$

MONTY'S RAW BAR
2550 S. Bayshore Dr., Coconut Grove: 305-856-3992
www.montysrawbar.com
CUISINE: American.
DRINKS: full bar.
SERVING: lunch, dinner.
This joint has been here forever. Back when the Grove was "the" place to be, it was one of the hottest tickets in town. Still offers casual waterfront indoor and outdoor dining. Seafood, sandwiches, salads and ribs while listening to live music and sitting on Biscayne Bay. $$$

TIGERTAIL + MARY
3321 Mary St, Coconut Grove, 305-722-5688
https://tigertailandmary.com
CUISINE: American (New)
DRINKS: Full bar
SERVING: Lunch and Dinner, Brunch
PRICE RANGE: $$$
Upscale neighborhood eatery here in the Grove with a clean, modern simple décor. I love the plants hanging from the shelves behind the bar, mixed in with bowls and bottles and jars Features a menu of American fare. Favorites: Tuna Crudo and Grilled Octopus. Indoor/Outdoor seating. Popular Brunch destination. Daily Happy Hour 5-7 p.m.

KEY BISCAYNE

If you find yourself on the Key, as we call it here in Miami, you could do worse than to drop into one of these nice eateries.

EL GRAN INKA
606 Crandon Blvd., Key Biscayne: 305 365-7883
http://www.graninka.com
CUISINE: Peruvian.
DRINKS: full bar.
SERVING: lunch, dinner.
You'd never know this was a chain (they have outlets in
Guatemala, El Salvador, Costa Rica, but in the USA, they
are only in Miami in 3 locations). Really good Peruvian
food. This is an upscale place, but there are other places
you can get great Peruvian food (see **Chalon's** on South
Beach) for a quarter the price point. $$$$

LIGHTHOUSE CAFÉ
1200 Crandon Blvd., Key Biscayne, 305-361-8487
www.lighthouserestaurants.com
CUISINE: Cafes
DRINKS: No Booze
SERVING: Breakfast-Lunch
PRICE RANGE: $$
NEIGHBORHOOD: Key Biscayne
Completely open-air eatery in Bill Bagg's Cape Florida
State Park, so make sure the weather's to your liking. Has
a large menu, salads, sandwiches, pastas and some Cuban

dishes (like pork chunks and black bean soup).There's a small fee to enter the park.

NOVECENTO
620 Crandon Blvd., Key Biscayne: 305 362-0900
http://www.novecento.com
CUISINE: Argentine steakhouse.
DRINKS: full bar.
SERVING: lunch, dinner.
Although to me this is basically an Argentine steakhouse (and it's really good), they say it's not just Argentine, but also Mediterranean and Pan Latin highlighted by French techniques. That the cuisine is not a fusion; rather each style is separate and is a pure reflection of its heritage. But to me, it's still an Argentine steakhouse. Indoor, outdoor.

RUSTY PELICAN
3201 Rickenbacker Causeway, Key Biscayne: 305 361-3818
www.therustypelican.com
CUISINE: American; seafood.
DRINKS: full bar.
SERVING: lunch, dinner daily.
Heavy on the seafood dishes, but what you really come here for is the spectacular view of downtown Miami. It's got an off-putting "corporate" feel to it and is huge (seats 400, but can do parties for 1,000). I always go on "off" days, and wouldn't be caught dead here on a Friday or Saturday night. But I know many people who love it when it's jammed. It's great for either lunch or dinner, depending on whether you want to look at the view in sunny daylight or romantic evenings. I even like it here on rainy, gusty days because I like looking out over the water when it's stormy. $$$

WHISKEY JOE'S BAR & GRILL
3301 Rickenbacker Cswy., Key Biscayne: 305-423-6590
www.whiskeyjoestampa.com/
CUISINE: American

DRINKS: Full Bar
SERVING: Lunch, Dinner
An offshoot of the original Tampa bar & grill, this location
has a Key West vibe serving everything from crab cake
sliders to mango salad with coconut shrimp. Live music.
$$

CHAPTER 4
NIGHTLIFE

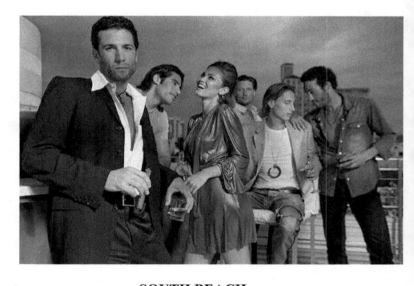

SOUTH BEACH
HOTEL LOBBY BARS - NIGHTCLUBS – BARS &
LOUNGES - DIVES – GAY BARS & CLUBS

THE MAINLAND
NIGHTCLUBS - MAINLAND
BARS & LOUNGES – MAINLAND

***

SOUTH BEACH

A night on the town means different things to different people: some people want to go to a nightclub, spend $300 for bottle service. For someone else, it's a stroll on the beach.

HOTEL LOBBY BARS

Most tourists usually only see the lobby of the hotel they're in. Unless a nightclub or lounge (like **Wall** in the **W**) is located in a hotel, they don't see other hotel lobbies.

Or—more to the point here—the bars in or off the lobbies that can be worth a trip in and of themselves.

One of the things I like to do when I'm entertaining out-of-towners is to take them on a **Hotel Lobby Bar Tour**. The idea is simple: select a list of four or five or six hotels and spend the evening moving from one to the other. Have a single drink in each, maybe an appetizer or two if you're peckish, and then get out and go on to the next one. You'll have had one of the best evenings of your visit. And you'll absorb quite a visual education on the glories of architectural design on South Beach—all for the (sometimes hefty) price of a drink.

It's essential to appreciate what the South Beach lobby bars are like (for comparison's sake) to make a short excursion (a ten-minute Uber / Lyft ride) up to the **Eden Roc** and the **Fontainebleau**, hotels next door to each other, both designed by the legendary architect **Morris Lapidus**, the man who once said, "Too much is never enough."

Walk through the lobby of the Fontainebleau first. It's quite expansive. Have a drink and then walk next door to the Eden Roc. These lobbies are stunning.

Then come back to South Beach and see what other designers have done to fully appreciate the over-the-top genius of Morris Lapidus.

THE DELANO
1685 Collins Ave., Miami Beach: 305-672-2000
www.delano-hotel.com
Enjoy the whimsical design brilliance of **Philippe Starck** as you walk through the lobby to the **Rose Bar**. When you get a load of his lobby interior here, you will understand the profound impact he has had on design around the world, and all the copycats that have mimicked his ideas. But I credit hotelier **Ian Schrager** for being even smarter and more talented than Starck: he hired him! Both Schrager and Starck have moved on from the Delano long ago, but their influence remains here to be seen and appreciated.

MONDRIAN
1100 West Ave., Miami Beach: 305-514-1500
www.mondrian-miami.com
Here you'll get a full sense of how strong Starck's influence is. Here it's all white, white and whiter. There's a stunning indoor bar, and this as well as the restaurant overlook the pool and Biscayne Bay. Outdoor bar as well. This is "Sunset Central," as it's the only hotel besides the Standard that faces west.

THE SAGAMORE
1671 Collins Ave., Miami Beach: 305-535-8088
www.sagamoresouthbeach.com
With 93 suites and two-story bungalows, the Sagamore is a bit big for a "boutique" hotel (though to be fair it does possess a boutique hotel's attention to service and detail). Not in question, however, is the inn's designation as an "Art Hotel."

THE SETAI
2001 Collins Ave., Miami Beach: 305-520-6000
www.thesetaihotel.com
The front half of this uber luxury inn is the '30s era
Dempsey Vanderbilt Hotel; remainder is a modern
glass tower that reaches up past the imagination. When
you enter the lobby bar in this place you leave South
Beach behind and move into a whole other dimension.

W SOUTH BEACH
2201 Collins Ave., Miami Beach: 305-938-3000
www.wsouthbeach.com
The Living Room Bar off the lobby will give you an idea
of what the big money buys in terms of design today.
Expect this place to be busy, because it's the Hot Spot this
year. If you're going for dinner, let the trendsetters trip
over themselves at **Mr. Chow** while you go to **Solea**, one
of the best true Spanish restaurants in town. Also home to
the uber-hip bottle club lounge, **Wall**.

THE VICTOR
1144 Ocean Dr., Miami Beach: 305-428-1234
www.hotelvictorsouthbeach.com

If you must hit Ocean Drive, then this is the place. Designed by the famed L. Murray Dixon in 1937 and retrofit by Parisian Jacques Garcia back in 2003 (to the reported tune of $48 million), the Victor's got both a charming lobby bar (V Bar) and a beautiful pool-with-a-view (Vue). And if you close your eyes you're on a classic ocean liner, and South Beach is as wondrous as ever. Take special note of the restored mural in the lobby.

NIGHTCLUBS

BASEMENT
2901 Collins Ave, Miami Beach, 786-257-4600
www.basementmiami.com
Located in the basement of **The Edition**, one of Miami Beach's hottest new hotels just a tad bit north of South Beach, this unique club was developed by Ian Schrager of Studio 54 offering music from Miami veteran Ben Pundole. A gathering spot for hipsters and those who aspire to be cool. Dress the part.

BODEGA TAQUERIA Y TEQUILA
1220 16th St, Miami Beach, 305-704-2145
www.bodegasouthbeach.com
Some come for the great Mexican street food (I come here with a Mexican who says the tacos are the best) but others come for the great bar scene located behind the door that looks like it leads to a port-a-potty. It actually leads down a short hallway to one of the hippest bars in Miami. This bar offers a relaxed atmosphere with friendly bartenders (a rarity these days) serving creative cocktails. Velvet couches, unique art, and a chill balcony. Pool table, DJs, and rowdy crowd, most of them with more tattoos than I

care to see, but the place is happening. I take visitors here, but it's not a place for an old fart like me to hang out.

LIV

Fontainebleau, 4441 Collins Ave., Miami Beach: 305-674-4680

www.livnightclub.com/

The Fontainebleau's signature hotspot may need no introduction, especially if you're familiar with the likes of **Tiesto** and **Cedric Gervais**. But wall-to-wall weekends of world-class DJs is only one of the reasons to trek up Collins and join the madding crowd; the other is Wednesday night's **Dirty Harry** party, which pits Miami's best spinners with some of the world's most out-there performers. Sure, it'll cost you. But some wild nights are well worth paying for.

NIKKI BEACH CLUB

1 Ocean Dr., Miami Beach: 305-538-1111

www.nikkibeach.com

What started out here at the foot of Ocean Drive now has outposts in places like Cabo San Lucas, Marbella, Cannes and all around the world. Full list of activities, but it's still a great place to lounge in the sun or play at night. And you're right on the beach, perfect for that nighttime walk with a moon over Miami. Dancing.

STORY

136 Collins Ave., Miami Beach: 305-538-2424

www.storymiami.com

I remember very well the nightclub Amnesia that once occupied this enormous space. Three levels of madness, all of it driven by heart-thumping music. Another outpost where $20 buys you a vodka cran.

B BAR
1440 Ocean Dr., Miami Beach: 305-531-6100
www.thebetsyhotel.com
Designed by Chi-town power broker **Callin Fortis**, of Big
Time Design Studios, the very same cat who brought the
wild world everything Crobar to Exit 66, B Bar is the
Betsy's basement playroom par excellence. And at equal
parts speakeasy and hide-out, it's one of the damn few
good reasons even to dare Ocean Drive anymore.

BROKEN SHAKER
Freehand Hotel, 2727 Indian Creek Dr, Miami Beach,
305-531-2727
www.thefreehand.com
Located in the backyard of the Freehand Hotel, formerly
the Indian Creek Hotel, that has now been transformed
into a hostel. Here you'll find the hostel's pool, herb
garden, bocce ball court, ping pong tables and outdoor
seating area. The crowd is friendly and there's often live
music. Small menu available.

THE CATALINA HOTEL & BEACH CLUB

1732 Collins Ave., Miami Beach: 305-674-1160
www.catalinasouthbeach.com.
Over the past couple years the Catalina has turned into a
sorta adult amusement park in its own right. There are the
joints: **Maxine's Bistro**, **Kung Fu Kitchen** and **Sushi,
Red Bar**. There are the pools: Bamboo and Rooftop. And
then there's the Bridge – now Verge – Art Fair, which
takes place each year at **Art Basel**. All in all, it's a
charming antidote to the mega-inns. And downright
affordable to boot.

KILL YOUR IDOL

222 Espanola Way, Miami Beach: 305-672-1852
www.killyouridol.com **WEBSITE DOWN AT
PRESSTIME**
Packed with pop culture artifacts such as a Playboy pinball
machine and a life-sized Bruce Lee, this sleek little hang
would be just what the locals ordered if she or he had any
say in the matter. Drinks are less than cheap, and if you're
hungry you can even grab food from The Alibi. And don't
forget to drop a dime in that jukebox. DJ Smeejay is often
seen bouncing the club in late hours.

LIVING ROOM - W HOTEL

2201 Collins Ave, Miami Beach, 305-938-3000
www.wsouthbeach.com/living-room-bar
Located in the lobby of W Hotel South Beach, this bar
specializes in custom made cocktails filled with natural
ingredients like fruits, herbs, & edible flowers. The drink
menu features infused, molecular mixology, and
innovative concoctions like the Electric Watermelon
(made with fresh watermelon, rosemary honey, peach
bitters, and bourbon then topped with honeydew caviar).
Drinks are pricey.

MOKAI

235 - 23rd St., Miami Beach: 786-735-3322
www.mokaimiami.com/
Now owned by The Opium Group, Mokai still retains
some of its storied hedonism. It just has a different accent.

MYNT

1921 Collins Ave., Miami Beach: 305-532-0727
www.myntlounge.com
Hot club serving locals and an international clientele. Big
stars come here: Mickey Rourke, Sean Penn, Jennifer
Lopez, Cameron Diaz, Britney Spears, Ricky Martin,
Jamie Foxx, Colin Farrell.

ROCKWELL

743 Washington Ave, Miami Beach: 305-793-3882
http://rockwellmiami.com/
This hip spot is the brainchild of former Liquid nightclub
owner Chris Paciello and is the hangout for celebs like
Justin Bieber and Sean Combs when they're in town.

SKYBAR
Shore Club
1901 Collins Ave., Miami Beach: 305-695-3100
www.shoreclub.com
Out by the pool you'll find the still-hot Skybar. Lots of
celebs and heavy lifters.

DIVE BARS

Well, there used to be a lot more of *these* (does anyone
remember **Jessie's Dollhouse Bar** on Washington
Avenue?), but gentrification and soaring rents have
squeezed a lot of colorful joints out of business. But a few
remain.

MAC'S CLUB DEUCE

222 14th St. (between Collins & Washington), Miami Beach: 305-531-6200

No web site, and certainly doesn't need one

The legendary dive bar where many scenes in "Miami Vice" were shot. The neon the crew put in was so cool owner **Mac Klein** left it up. (Mac celebrated his 100th birthday in 2015 and I was there. He died a year later at 101.) In this dive, which his family still operates the way Mac did, Happy Hour starts at 8 (ahem, that's 8 a.m., and runs till 7 p.m.). Regular patron "Persian Jimmy" used to say: "If you can't get drunk in eleven hours, you're not tryin'." A must visit. Buy a T-shirt.

FINNEGAN'S 2

942 Lincoln Rd., Miami Beach: 305-538-7997

www.finnegansbars.com **WEBSITE DOWN AT PRESS TIME**

Sports bar with lots of TVs. Pub fare. Low prices. The only real dive bar on Lincoln Road. ☹

I used to think the food here was awful, but I got stuck there one night in the rain and the chicken wings and French fries were to die for!

TED'S HIDEAWAY
124 Second St., Miami Beach: 305-532-9869
A dive bar where you can find pool tables, beer and booze and girl bartenders from places like Romania, Russia, Bulgaria. The owner's drinks are a little skimpy, kinda like the outfits he makes the girls wear. He's so cheap he doesn't even have a web site, not that you'd need one for this joint. A little sandier than the **Deuce**, and a little shadier too. So what? Open daily 8am-5am. One of my favorites.

GAY BARS / CLUBS

Gone are the days when the big gay clubs provided that indefinable spark that ignited the South Beach nightlife scene and made it explode. The best "gay" clubs (**Warsaw Ballroom**—it ran from 1989 to 1998 and **Paragon**, from March 1992 to 1994, attracted a heady mix of gay *and* straight people, but they were all people "on the edge," at the forefront of whatever was happening. Add to this mix that the White Party was the first and most lavish party among the international gay **Circuit parties**, and you had a combustible environment.

It's waaaay different now. The cover at the Warsaw was $5. There was a tiny VIP Room upstairs. But mostly anybody could get into it. Money didn't matter. No bottle service. No attitude.

The reputation that South Beach is a huge gay Mecca lingers on and can't be shaken. But there's actually only a handful of gay bars on South Beach.

GAYTHERING
1409 Lincoln Rd, Miami Beach, 786-284-1176
www.gaythering.com
This bar is located in the cozy lobby of Miami Beach's
only "straight friendly" hotel. Located where trendy
Lincoln Road meets Biscayne Bay. It's a sleek bar with a
friendly staff, craft cocktails, upscale ambience.

TWIST
1057 Washington Ave., Miami Beach: 305-538-9478.
www.twistsobe.com/
South Beach's famous long-running gay bar, where
everybody goes after 3 a.m. to revel in what's left of the
old decadence. (This is where the staffs of the other gays
bars end up between 3 and 5 a.m.) They might have called
this place the Last Chance Saloon because if you can't
pick up someone here, you're really not trying very hard.

NIGHTCLUBS MAINLAND

CHURCHILL'S PUB
5501 NE 2nd Ave., Miami: 305-757-1807
http://churchillspub.com
Up in Little Haiti, this joint (and it *is* a joint) offers live underground music. Been here since 1979. Indie music is the scene here.

EL PALENQUE NIGHTCLUB
1115 NW 22nd Ave., Miami: 305-644-7376
No web site at presstime
Well-known Mexican bands featured monthly. Other weekends, DJ Turko mans the turntables, playing bachata, salsa, and merengue on Fridays, open format on Saturdays, and primarily Mexican music on Sundays. Nightly, a sexy dance contest. Patrons vote on the girl with the best presentation. 5 beers for $18. Also bar food. Sometimes a cover, depending on entertainment.

SPACE
34 NE 11th St., Miami: 786-357-6456
http://clubspace.com
Big-time DJs and dancing is the scene here in this massive club. For the hard-partying set. Make sure your girlfriend doesn't get kidnapped and sold into slavery when everybody's so drunk they won't notice.

BARS & LOUNGES

THE ANDERSON MIAMI
709 NE 79th St., Miami, 305-757-3368

www.theandersonmiami.com
Located right off Biscayne Blvd, this hipster hangout
(formerly Magnum's) is a combination of indoor and
outdoor areas. The inside features a long dark bar area
with great music and even a menu of snacks (from Fried
chicken sandwich to TexMex). This new interpretation of
an old theme offers a cleaner, hipper party atmosphere but
the piano and dance floor remain.

THE BAR AT LEVEL 25
Conrad Hotel
1395 Brickell Ave., Miami - 305-503-6529
http://conradhotels1.hilton.com
Level 25 indicates that this bar is on the 25th floor, and
worth a trip just to get a gander at the stunning view from
this height. Best time to go is weekday happy-hour when
prices drop to a reasonable $5 to $8. Later, prices go way
up. Free valet parking (at least). Food served all day and
night. (Try the tempura-battered soft-shell crab with spicy
chipotle aioli.)

BLUE MARTINI
900 S Miami Ave #250, Miami - 305-981-2583
http://bluemartinilounge.com
42 versions of the martini. This spot fills up with yuppies
from nearby Brickell Avenue offices, but still a good-
looking crowd. No one here didn't go to college. The
servers are young and attractive, the bar food better than
average. In Mary Brickell Village downtown. Happy hour
specials; cover charge (if you can believe it) Friday and
Saturday nights.

CHURCHILL'S PUB
5501 NE 2nd Ave., Miami: 305-757-1807
www.churchillspub.com

Place in Little Haiti that was here (from 1979) *before* there was a Little Haiti. Little Haiti just sort of grew up around Churchill's. I always find it funny to go over here, walk into the place, and find *white* people. Big supporter of the indie music scene, punk rock, etc.

THE CORNER
1035 N Miami Ave, Miami, 305-961-7887
www.thecornermiami.com/
Located in downtown's entertainment district (next door to Club Space), this charming nightspot offers a variety of interesting cocktails that you won't find next door. Here you'll find a modern-day saloon atmosphere and cocktails served with natural ingredients. This bar also boasts a nice selection of craft beers on draft, a price-conscious wine list and an impressive late-night menu.

EL PATIO WYNWOOD
167 NW 23 St, Miami, 786-409-2241
www.elpatiowynwood.com
Outdoor spot that is definitely part of the scene. Great specials (4 beers for $4? Bring it on). Lots of seating but it's all outdoors. Some of it is covered – some not. Nice selection of beers and crafted cocktails. Variety of tunes play depending on the DJ. Live bands usually play Latin music.

VAGABOND HOTEL LOUNGE/BAR
7301 Biscayne Blvd, Miami, 305-400-8420
www.thevagabondhotelmiami.com
Step back in time at relive the old Miami experience at the reopened Vagabond Hotel. This is one of my favorite spots in Miami. Lounge by the poolside bar – a mix of vintage Miami and Palm Springs. Great happy hour on weekends and affordable cocktails. (The restaurant is really good, too.)

CHAPTER 5

COUNTY BEACHES

SOUTH BEACH ATTRACTIONS

MUSEUMS

MAINLAND ATTRACTIONS / TOURS

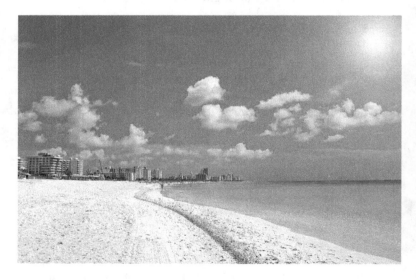

THE BEACHES

You did come here for the beaches, right? Well, assuming you did, you have to know there *are* other beaches besides South Beach, thank you very much. Here are my favorites:

BAL HARBOUR BEACH
Collins Ave. - 96th St. to Haulover Inlet, Bal Harbour: 305/947-3525
www.BalHarbourFlorida.com
Palm-shaded jogging path curves around mile-long beach. Jetty (with fishing permitted) at north end of beach. Limited metered parking lot available beneath Haulover Bridge. No lifeguards or showers.

BILL BAGGS CAPE FLORIDA STATE BEACH
1200 S. Crandon Blvd., Key Biscayne: 305/361-5811
http://www.FloridaStateParks.org
A very scenic beach at the southern tip of Key Biscayne. Walking and bicycle trails wind through native vegetation. Historic lighthouse and food concession. Restrooms, picnic tables and shower facilities available. Parking fee.

CRANDON PARK BEACH
4000 Crandon Blvd., Key Biscayne: 305/361-5421
www.miamidade.gov/parks/parks/crandon_beach.asp
Three-mile long lagoon style beach protected by 13 lifeguard towers. Beach wheelchairs for rent. Children's carrousel, playgrounds and picnic areas. Ideal for families. Shower facilities, restrooms, shelters and lifeguards. Parking fee.

HAULOVER BEACH PARK / NUDE BEACH / GAY NUDE BEACH
10800 Collins Ave., Miami Beach: 305/947-3525
http://www.miamidade.gov/parks/haulover.asp
Spacious beach with shady picnic area/barbecue grills near the dunes. Beach wheelchairs for rent. Pedestrian tunnels

link to the park and marina on Biscayne Bay. Nine-hole golf course, tennis courts, kite flying area and kite shop. Clothing-optional section at northern end, with the gay section farthest north. Parking fee.

MIAMI BEACH/SOUTH POINTE PARK
Ocean Dr. at 5th St., Miami Beach: 305/673-7779
www.miamibeachfl.gov
Entrance through the park at 1 Washington Ave. Beach located at the southern tip of South Beach. Great place to watch cruise ships sailing out to sea. Parking fee.

MIAMI BEACH – SOUTH BEACH
Ocean Drive & 5th St. to Collins Ave. & 21st St., Miami Beach: 305/673-7714
www.miamibeachfl.gov
Entrance anywhere there is a public access walkway.

MIAMI BEACH – CENTRAL
Collins Ave. - 21st St. to 46th St., Miami Beach: 305/673-7714
www.miamibeachfl.gov
Raised boardwalk over the dunes popular for strolling and jogging. Proximity to sidewalk cafes along Collins Avenue. Lifeguard towers, food/drink concessions, beach chair/umbrella rentals. Parking fee.

SURFSIDE BEACH
Collins Ave. from 88th St. to 96th St., Surfside
www.townofsurfsidefl.gov
Facilities are available in 93rd St. Community Center for fee.

VIRGINIA KEY BEACH – NORTH
North of Rickenbacker Cswy. At Crandon Blvd., Key Biscayne: 305/575-5256

www.virginiakeybeachpark.net
Windsurfing and ultra light seaplane rental. Great views of
Brickell Avenue and downtown Miami skyline.
Food/drink concessions, restroom. Parking fee.

VIRGINIA KEY BEACH – SOUTH
South of Rickenbacker Causeway, Key Biscayne:
305/361-2833
www.virginiakeybeachpark.net
Ultra-secluded beach close to Key Biscayne. Shady areas,
nature trails and a bird sanctuary nearby. Only beach in
Miami-Dade County where dogs on leashes are allowed.

SOUTH BEACH
ATTRACTIONS

FOR THE TOURIST
A few suggestions to keep you busy when you're not at the
beach, not in a club, not in a restaurant and not shopping:

SPECIFIC INFORMATION DURING YOUR VISIT.
Check out the listings in the weekly newspaper *New
Times*, which has boxes on every corner, or use your
laptop (or increasingly these days, even your cellphone)
and go to their web site, www.miaminewtimes.com. The
Miami Herald only has a good list in its Friday edition.
But they also have comprehensive listings online at
www.miamiherald.com.

ART DECO TOURS
South Beach Art Deco District, 305-814-4058
www.artdecotours.com
Enrich your visit to South Beach with an enlightening
walking tour of the famed Art Deco district. Transport in
time to the '20's, '30's and beyond. Learn about the

colorful history and admire unique architecture and design with exclusive access to interiors and rooftops. Tours great for families. Other tours available: Little Havana and Art Deco Cocktail Tour – historical tour with cocktails.

CHAMBER OF COMMERCE
1920 Meridian Ave., Miami Beach: 305-674-1300. www.miamibeachchamber.com. Has lots of listings on its web site to help you plan your trip.

OFFICIAL ART DECO GIFT SHOP & WALKING TOURS
10th Street & Ocean Dr., Miami Beach: 305-531-3484 Also: 305-672-2014. Organized by the Miami Design Preservation League
www.mdpl.org
They have a very interesting 90-minute walking tour that provides an introduction to the Art Deco, Mediterranean Revival, and Miami Modern (MiMo) styles found within the Miami Beach Architectural Historic District. Explore hotels, restaurants, and other commercial structures with a visit to a number of interiors. Tours depart from the Art Deco Gift Shop on the following schedule: Daily at 10:30am (except Thursday, 6:30pm). Reservation not needed. Just show up at the Art Deco Gift Shop 10 minutes of the scheduled departure time in order to purchase your ticket, $20. (Verify this by phone before you go.)

BIKE RENTALS & TOURS
210 – 10th St. (Collins Ave. and 10th St.), Miami Beach: 305-604-0001 / www.bikeandroll.com

BOTANICAL GARDENS
2000 Convention Center Dr., Miami Beach: 305-673-7256. www.mbgarden.org. A restful place (OK, it's a little

dull) in a very un-restful city, tucked ingloriously in a nook between the parking lot adjacent to the Convention Center and the Dade Canal marking the northernmost point of South Beach. A three-minute walk north of Lincoln Road.

COLONY THEATRE
1040 Lincoln Rd., Miami Beach: 305-674-1040
http://miaminewdrama.org/
www.colonymb.org
Check to see exactly what's playing in this little Art Deco theatre on Lincoln Road. **Miami New Drama** is the resident theatre company here, and they always have provocative productions. It's an architectural gem inside and out. I actually had one of my plays produced here. Naturally, it sold out.

DUCK (WATER & LAND) TOURS
1661 James Ave., Miami Beach: 305-673-2217
www.ducktoursmiami.com
Leaving from the heart of South Beach, these amphibious vehicles provide a once in a lifetime journey (90 minutes) of the famous Miami landmarks before a dramatic "Splashdown" into Biscayne Bay for a close up look at the many homes of the "Rich & Famous" on Star Island. Soon after your journey on a Miami Duck Tour begins, you will quickly realize that you are engaged in an interactive performance that far exceeds your standard tour expectations. Each tour guide has a background in acting/comedy to ensure a highly entertaining experience for each passenger complete with jokes, music, plenty of interaction and of course "quacking." Don't let all of that joking around fool you; each guide at Miami Duck Tours takes their knowledge of the Magic City very seriously. (I took this from their web site. I've never actually been on this little trip.)

ESPAÑOLA WAY

Española Way is quaintly referred to by tourism officials as "a historic Spanish village" (actually, it's a single street located in the area bounded by 14th and 15th Streets and Washington and Jefferson avenues on South Beach. The street has recently reopened after a $2.5 million restoration.). But it's still worth strolling down and having lunch or dinner. For South Beach, it really is quaint. With Mediterranean Revival buildings dating back to the 1920s

FILLMORE AT THE GLEASON THEATRE

1700 Convention Center Dr., Miami Beach: 305-673-7300.
http://fillmoremb.com/

FISHING

300 Alton Rd., Miami Beach Marina: 305-372-9470.
www.fishingmiami.com

They have a big boat that takes a crowd out to go fishing. But they also act as booking agents for many charter boats, skiff guides, flats guides and back country guides. Give them a call with what you are looking for and they'll get it done for you. They can also arrange sightseeing. They have the only blue water sightseeing vessel for up to 103 passengers in South Florida.

FROST SCIENCE MUSEUM

1101 Biscayne Blvd, Miami, 305-434-9600
www.frostscience.org
ADMISSION: Nominal fee
NEIGBORHOOD: Downtown
A science museum, planetarium, and aquarium located in Museum Park in downtown Miami that opened in 2017.

To be perfectly honest, this place is strictly for kids. An adult quickly gets bored. The Planetarium has quite an interesting show, but unless you have kids you want ot amuse for a while, skip it. The museum is divided into four buildings: Frost Planetarium, Aquarium, and North and West Wings. The three-level aquarium may be the star attraction of this venue but it's also a learning and hands-on museum with lots of interactive exhibits. Learn the core science behind living systems, the solar system and known universe, the physics of flight, light and lasers, the biology of the human body and mind, and more. The "learning exhibits" are so elementary as to boggle the mind. The 250,000 square foot museum sits on four acres within the waterfront Museum Park across from PAMM (Perez Art Museum Miami).

KAYAK RENTALS & TOURS
1771 Purdy Ave., Miami Beach: 305-975-5087
www.southbeachkayak.com/
It's a little tough to find this place. It's tucked away over on the last road before you cross the Venetian Causeway But it's right across the street from the Sunset Harbour Marina so you can slip into the water very quickly.

LINCOLN ROAD
www.lincolnroad.org
As Ocean Drive has become more "touristy," Lincoln
Road has taken up the slack as a place more frequented by
locals. The web site has all the stores, shops, restaurants.
The architect that created the Fontainebleau and the Eden
Roc (Morris Lapidus), conjured up the fanciful shapes
strewn along the center of Lincoln Road. They are worth a
second look as you move down the street.

MIAMI BEACH GOLF CLUB
2301 Alton Rd., Miami Beach: 305-532-3350
www.miamibeachgolfclub.com
Originally opened as Bayshore Golf Course in 1923 as part
of pioneering developer Carl Fisher's ambitious Alton
Beach subdivision that was designed to lure wealthy
winter residents from New York, Indianapolis and Detroit,
this professional course is now owned by the city.

MIAMI CITY BALLET
2200 Liberty Ave., Miami Beach: 305-929-7000

www.miamicityballet.org. One of America's most acclaimed ballet companies. If you're in town when they are performing, you owe it to yourself to spend an evening with them.

NEW WORLD SYMPHONY
500 – 17th St., Miami Beach: 305-673-3330
www.nws.edu
NWS, America's "orchestra academy," is housed in a stunning new (2011) Frank Gehry-designed concert hall at the corner of 17th Street and Washington Avenue, just north of Lincoln Road. Students from NWS leave to populate the great orchestras all over the world. Try to work in a concert if you're in town during their season, because it's a real treat you won't find anywhere else in the world (and you get a good look inside Gehry's new architectural wonder).

OOLITE ARTS
924 Lincoln Rd., Miami Beach: 305-674-8278
www.oolitearts.org

The buildings housing Oolite Arts have been converted into a warren of tiny studios where several dozen artists working on all media do their thing. Artists you'd never get to see (because the rents are so high on Lincoln Road) get to show their wares, and you get to watch them paint, watch them sculpt, meet them, and if you like what you see, even buy their work. Definitely worth a walk-through.

SOUTH POINTE PARK
1 Washington Ave., Miami Beach: 305-673-7779
http://web.miamibeachfl.gov/
At the very southern tip of Miami Beach overlooking Government Cut, the inlet leading to the Port of Miami. Great place to go on Friday or Saturday afternoons to watch the cruise ships head out in a stately procession as they begin their trips to the Caribbean. Only problem with this place: after spending millions "improving" this park, they removed *every single shade tree* from the western half of the park, so it's unbearably hot half the year. Very inhospitable place. You don't know whether to shoot the talentless designers or the incredibly incompetent city planning officials who approved this abortion.

TOURIST HOTLINE: 305-673-7400. Can usually steer you in the right direction.

THE VILLA CASA CASUARINA (Versace Mansion)
1114 Ocean Dr., Miami Beach: 786-485-2200
www.vmmiamibeach.com
Poor Peter Loftin. Well, not exactly "poor" Peter Loftin.
He's the North Carolina gazillionaire who bought the villa
on Ocean Drive where Versace was notoriously gunned
down by Andrew Cunanan. He's turned it into a private
club, a hotel, an events location, but nothing worked.
Finally, in 2013, he sold it to the family that owns the
Jordache fashion line. (Has anyone noticed the irony?)
What they ought to do is turn it into a museum, so people
could go inside to see how Versace lived. I've been to
many events and dinners inside, and it's quite the little
pleasure palace. He lived well. Currently The Villa Casa
Casuarina is open as an upscale hotel and the restaurant is
open to the public.

WATER TOURS
OCEAN FORCE ADVENTURES
Miami Beach Marina, 300 Alton Rd., Miami Beach: 305-
372-3388 www.Oceanforceadventures.com. Experience
the excitement of a Zodiac RIB ride (these are the same
boats used by the FBI, special military forces, DEA and
Coast Guard) on their 2-hour outdoor adventure

sightseeing boat tours as you speed across brilliant blue ocean waters and soak up the sun-drenched Florida skies to explore the glamour, the mystery and the history of Miami Beach and Biscayne Bay. Their boat is docked at the center dock directly behind the main entrance to the marina.

CRUISE SHIP DEPARTURE SPECTACLE
Although it's not what you'd call an official "attraction," it's still one of the best things to do if you're visiting South Beach on a Friday or Saturday. These are the two days the ocean liners head out to the Caribbean with their boatloads of people who sail right by South Beach without ever knowing what they're missing. You get a pretty good view of exclusive Fisher Island across the Cut and the ferries that take cars and people over there. If you don't mind spending a few bucks (well, quite a few bucks), go early (say, 4pm) and get a table outside at **Smith and Wollensky's** and have their fabulous cold seafood platter or one of their great steaks and watch as the ships go by. Or just nurse a drink at the bar and you'll get the same experience without the high cost. If you're really broke, sit on the rocks under the shade of the seagrape trees hugging the Cut and enjoy it all for free!

HOTEL LOBBY TOUR

See the opening section of the **Nightlife** chapter for a rundown on my favorite hotel lobbies.

MUSEUMS

WOLFSONIAN MUSEUM
1001 Washington Ave., Miami Beach: 305-531-1001
www.wolfsonian.org

One of the most unusual museums in the world, it was founded by the mercurial millionaire Micky Wolfson. His fascinating collection of objects from the modern era (1885-1945) focuses on how art and design shape and reflect the human experience. Some of the things Micky collected you won't believe. (Ask them where the toasters are.) Florida Int'l University now operates the museum. There's even a little café in here that's quite a find and worth a trip on its own. Free museum tours every Friday evening at 6 p.m.

HOLOCAUST MEMORIAL
1933 Meridian Ave., Miami Beach: 305-538-1663. http://holocaustmemorialmiamibeach.org Right behind the Botanical Gardens, across from the same parking lot, you'll find this poignant memorial to the Holocaust. Don't rush through this open-air exhibit. (Chamber of Commerce is across the street where you can grab stacks of brochures.)

WILZIG EROTIC ART MUSEUM
1205 Washington Ave., Miami Beach: 305-532-9336. www.weam.com. All the kinds of forbidden art previously hidden from public view. (Well, until the Internet came along.) Honestly, this place sounds like something so tacky you'd never give it a second thought, but I was finally persuaded to visit the place, and it has thousands of museum-quality items that will really impress you. My reaction to the world-class collection assembled here is exactly the opposite of what I imagined it would be. So, give it a shot.

JEWISH MUSEUM OF FLORIDA
301 Washington Ave., Miami Beach: 305-672-5044. www.jewishmuseum.com. Unique destination for people of every age and background. Site comprised of two

former synagogues, on the National Register of Historic Places, restored by the Museum, and connected with a glass-domed bistro. Core exhibit, *MOSAIC*, depicts 250 years of Jewish Life in Florida, a story of one immigrant group that is generic for all families. Enjoy at least two more changing history or art exhibits, films and their Museum Store. Museum open 10-5 Tuesdays-Sundays, closed Civil & Jewish Holidays; free on Saturdays. Wheelchair accessible and parking in vicinity.

ART TOURS

Ever since **Art Basel** selected South Beach for its Western Hemisphere art fair (instead of, say, someplace sensible like New York), all of Miami has become an international hub of artistic activity. And the really big money rolls into town the first of December to buy and sell. And it's big, Big, BIG!

And it's all of Miami, not just South Beach. The frenzied activity has poured across the causeways to Miami's Wynwood and Design districts, full of mostly empty warehouses anyway, with developers begging for something to happen in a moribund and speculative economy.

Developers like **Craig Robins, Tony Goldman** and **Martin Margulies** opened HUGE warehouses and collected art themselves with wild abandon. (This was during that period when anybody with money began collecting art because it was fashionable, not because the "art" was necessarily any good.)

So the town was ripe for a cataclysmic shake up.

Art Basel in Miami has become the most interesting and exciting art fair in the world in just a few short years, easily eclipsing its sponsor and eponymous creator, Art Basel in Switzerland, for sizzle and fun.

Art Basel had another energizing effect: it shook up the torpid Miami museum scene, if indeed there really had been one before. Now, area museums have spruced up, expanded, brought in curators and directors of higher stature.

So, if you have any interest in real art, do some research and take some time to explore the many offerings.

MAINLAND ATTRACTIONS

BISCAYNE NATIONAL PARK
9700 SW 328th St., Homestead: 305 230-7275
www.nps.gov/bisc
A 53-foot glass-bottom boat and a 45-foot diving and snorkeling catamaran takes you across southern Biscayne Bay, through wilderness, mangrove creeks, islands, and out to tropical coral reefs teeming with sea life. Family snorkeling and scuba diving available from the boat. Canoe and kayak rentals, picnic area, walking trails, fishing, camping and shower facilities available. Reservations required. Waterfront visitor center offers exhibits, films and information. Open daily 8 a.m.-5:30p.m. Visitor Center open daily 8:30 a.m.-5 p.m. Glass-bottom boat tour: adults $24.45, children (12 and under) $16.45, seniors (62 and over) $19.45. Scuba diving $54, snorkeling: adults $35, children (12 and under) $29.95. Glass-bottom boat departs at 10 a.m., scuba/family snorkel departs at 1:30 p.m. Scuba diving departs at 8:30 a.m.

BISCAYNE NATURE CENTER
Marjory Stoneman Douglas Biscayne Nature Center
6767 Crandon Blvd., Key Biscayne: 305 361-6767, ext. 119. www.biscaynenaturecenter.org
Offers hands-on marine exploration, coastal hammock hikes, fossil-rock reef walks, local history lectures and beach walks. Marine exploration trips scheduled at low

tide only. All trips led by naturalist guide. Reservations required. Call for tour information and reservations.

COOPERTOWN AIRBOAT RIDES
22700 SW 8th St., Miami-305 226-6048
www.coopertownairboats.com
Offering airboat rides and alligator exhibitions since 1945. Professional guides lead tours through Hardwood Hammock to see wildlife in its native Everglades environment. Just 11 miles west of Florida' s Turnpike. Gift shop and restaurant with a menu that includes frog legs and gator tail. Call ahead to book a private tour. Open daily 8 a.m.-7 p.m.

CORAL CASTLE MUSEUM
28655 S. Dixie Highway, Homestead-305-248-6345
www.coralcastle.com
This quirky monument is one of Greater Miami's more unusual attractions. Giant pieces of coral rock were carved into a variety of objects by Edward Leedskalnin in the 1920s, as a tribute to unrequited love. The construction techniques behind this mystery garden of fantastic coral sculptures continue to baffle experts and visitors. This attraction has been featured in hundreds of newspaper and magazine articles.

CORAL GABLES MERRICK HOUSE
907 Coral Way, Coral Gables: 305 460-5391
www.coralgables.com
This is the boyhood home of George E. Merrick, founder and developer of the City of Coral Gables. This historic landmark originally began as an 1899 frame house, and was added onto in 1907. The house has been restored to the 1920s period and filled with the Merrick family's art, furniture and personal treasures. The park is open to the public on Wednesdays and Sundays for guided tours at 1,

2 and 3 p.m. Suggested admission, which includes the guided tour, is $5 for adults, $3 for seniors/students/group tours, $1 for children ages 6-12, and free for children under 5 years old.

DOLPHIN HARBOR
Miami Seaquarium
4400 Rickenbacker Causeway , Miami- 305-361-5705
www.miamiseaquarium.com
This new facility allows visitors to slip into a wet suit and for an up-close adventure with dolphins. With two different programs there is something for everyone. For the ride of a lifetime, enjoy the Dolphin Odyssey, a deep-water experience including a dorsal tow on one of the dolphins. Or book a Dolphin Encounter, a shallow-water experience where guests touch, feed and play with the dolphins. Looking for more of a behind the scenes experience, enroll to be Trainer for a Day. In this day-long program, guests experience how the facility keeps these marine mammals healthy and happy, plus enjoy a Dolphin Odyssey and get up close with the sea lions.

DRAGONFLY EXPEDITIONS

1825 Ponce de Leon Blvd., Suite 369, Coral Gables-305
774-9019

www.dragonflyexpeditions.com

These purveyors of uncommon adventures provide award-winning, distinctive group day and half-day journeys through the Everglades and Miami's colorful history for the sophisticated traveler.

EVERGLADES ALLIGATOR FARM

40351 SW 192nd Ave., Florida City: 305-247-2628

www.everglades.com

Explore the Everglades on a thrilling airboat tour and enjoy live shows every hour featuring alligators and snakes. Open daily 9 a.m.-6 p.m. Adults $23 for farm, airboat ride and shows; children $15.50 for farm, airboat ride and shows; Adults farm admission only $15.50; children farm admission only $10.50.

EVERGLADES NATIONAL PARK

305-242-7799; www.nps.gov/ever/

There are several ways to get into the Everglades, so we strongly recommend you look over their web site to decide which way you want to experience this place. There's nothing else in the world like Everglades National Park, the largest subtropical wilderness in the United States, boasting rare and endangered species. It has been designated a World Heritage Site, International Biosphere Reserve, and Wetland of International Importance, significant to all people of the world. The fact that Big Sugar continues to pollute it and kill off hundreds of species with the collusion of both the Federal and State governments is another story, so we strongly urge you to see what's left of it while you can! It really ought to be seen in the summer, when it's rainy season, but then it's also most uncomfortable (those pesky mosquitoes). In the dry winter, the place is rather parched, so it doesn't have the same effect on you.

EVERGLADES SAFARI PARK
26700 Tamiami Trail (SW 8th Street), Miami-305 226-6923
www.evergladessafaripark.com
The park features an alligator farm and show, guided airboat rides, a jungle trail, an interpretive center, a restaurant and a gift shop. Private tours are available. Open daily 8:30 a.m.-5 p.m. Adults $20, children (5-11) $10, children (under 5) free.

FAIRCHILD TROPICAL BOTANIC GARDEN
10901 Old Cutler Road, Coral Gables-305 667-1651
www.fairchildgarden.org
This premier conservation and education-based garden and recognized international leader in conservation is dedicated to exploring, explaining and conserving the world of tropical plants. It houses the National Palm Collection, has the world's greatest living collection of palms and cycads; an education program reaching more than 30,000 school children per year; hosts popular events like the International Mango and Orchid Festivals, the Ramble, concerts, affiliated plant society shows and sales; and is a not-for-profit organization relying on the support of its 40,000 members and benefactors. It hosts major events such as Les Lalanne at Fairchild in 2010 and 2011.

FROST MUSEUM OF SCIENCE
1101 Biscayne Blvd, Miami, 305-434-9600
www.frostscience.org
ADMISSION: Nominal fee
NEIGBORHOOD: Downtown
A science museum, planetarium, and aquarium located in Museum Park in downtown Miami that opened in 2017.

The museum is divided into four buildings: Frost Planetarium, Aquarium, and North and West Wings. The three-level aquarium may be the star attraction of this venue but it's also a learning and hands-on museum with lots of interactive exhibits. Learn the core science behind living systems, the solar system and known universe, the physics of flight, light and lasers, the biology of the human body and mind, and more. The 250,000 square foot museum sits on four acres within the waterfront Museum Park across from **PAMM (Perez Art Museum Miami)**. Except for the Planetarium, I found the whole thing pretty much of a bore, with the exhibits scaled down to the understanding of small children. You can do the whole place in an hour (except for the Planetarium show).

FRUIT & SPICE PARK
24801 SW 187th Ave., Homestead: 305-247-5727
www.redlandfruitandspice.com/
Established in 1944, this tropical paradise is nestled in the heart of the Redland District, just 35 miles south of Downtown Miami. More than 500 varieties of exotic fruits, herbs, spices and nuts from throughout the world are found in this lush 39-acre park. Open daily except Christmas Day 9 a.m.-5 p.m. Guided tours conducted daily on a tour tram at 11, 1:30 and 3, and are included in the price of admission. Adults $6, children (6-12) $1.50, under 6 free. Gift shop on site. Picnic facilities available.

GLOBAL AIR GROUP
603 SW 77th Way, Pembroke Pines, 954-605-8155 / 954-639-4010
www.tourhelicopter.com
This one is centrally located in downtown Miami – you actually have to take a short boat ride from their dock in

Bayside Marina to their floating helipad in the Bay. Close
to South Beach.

GO MIAMI CARD
Miami Beach Visitor Center
Miami Beach Convention Center - 800-887-9103
http://www.gomiamicard.com
Miami's multi-attraction pass featuring more than 40
Miami area attractions plus discounts on shopping and
dining. Customers may choose from one, two, three, five
or seven days of unlimited admission to Miami's very best
attractions, museums, tours and cruises, and have two
weeks to use it. The card gives visitors the ultimate tailor-
made destination experience at a great value. Attractions
include Miami Seaquarium, Jungle Island, Duck Tours and
many more.

GRAY LINE MIAMI
Miami: 877-643-1258
www.graylinemiami.com
This company has 100 years of tradition and history and
operates in 150 destinations around the world. Offering
travelers and their representatives the full range of
inbound/receptive tour operator services: sightseeing tours,
private charter transportation that gives individual and
group travelers the opportunity to stay and enjoy the many
amazing and unique features that South Florida has to
offer. Now operating Gray Line signature Miami
Sightseeing Hop On-Hop Off.

HAULOVER BEACH PARK / NUDE BEACH
10800 Collins Ave., Bal Harbour: 305-947-3525 /
www.miamidade.gov/parks/parks/haulover_park.asp
Has one of the most beautiful beaches – a mile and a half
stretch. Open ocean surf, various shaded picnic facilities,
beautifully landscaped sand dunes, and concession stands.

The beach is ideal for surfing as well as swimming. Guarded by well-trained lifeguards. Across the street from the beach, Haulover Park has a full-service marina, restaurant, tennis courts, family 9-hole golf course, sundries shop and kite shops. The northern portion of this beach is for nudists.

HELICOPTER TOURS
There's more than one service: click below to go to individual listings in this chapter:
Global Air
Miami Executive Helicopters

HISTORICAL MUSEUM OF SOUTHERN FLORIDA
101 W. Flagler St., Miami: 305-375-1492
http://www.hmsf.org
Although this beautiful facility is tucked in the middle of what constitutes "downtown Miami," it's still worth a trek, even though it's a pain in the ass to get to if you're a tourist, requiring a bus or a $20-$25 cab ride.
The Historical Museum of Southern Florida tells the stories of South Florida and the Caribbean. It's one of the largest private, regional history museums in the country.

ISLAND QUEEN CRUISES
Bayside Marketplace, 401 Biscayne Blvd., Miami, 305 379-5119

www.islandqueencruises.com

Sit back and relax for an unforgettable bilingual narrated sightseeing cruise along scenic Biscayne Bay. See Miami's spectacular coastal sites including the beautiful Downtown Miami skyline, the Port of Miami, Fisher Island, Miami Beach and "Millionaire's Row" - the homes of the rich and famous. Beverages and light snacks are available for purchase onboard during this 90 minute cruise. All of their modern yachts feature an air-conditioned lower salon, enclosed in picture windows, as well as an upper-deck where guests may take in the fresh ocean breeze under a protective awning. Please arrive at their ticket booth 30 minutes prior to departure to receive boarding passes. Departs every hour on the hour from 11 a.m. to 7 p.m., every day.

KITEBOARDING

6767 Crandon Blvd., Key Biscayne, 305-345-9974
www.miamikiteboarding.com

You actually have to learn how to fly a kite before you become a kiteboarder. You will need several hours of lessons.

MIAMI CULINARY TOURS

1000 5th St., Suite 200, Miami Beach: 786-942-8856
www.miamiculinarytours.com

This company offers the South Beach Food Tour and the Little Havana Food Tour. Both tours provide a non-touristy, local experience so attendees get the opportunity to immerse themselves into the local culture, and feel and eat like a native. The tours blend a historical, architectural and cultural experience together with an intimate, behind-the-scenes culinary introduction to savor the best cuisine the area has to offer - all at an affordable price.

MIAMI EXECUTIVE HELICOPTERS
Tamiami Airport
14150 SW 129 St., 786-507-5200
www.miamiheli.com
Take friends and family on a one-of-a-kind helicopter
adventure over Miami. The helicopter travels just a few
hundred feet off the ground over the coastline of Key
Biscayne, Viscaya Museum & Gardens, Brickell,
Downtown Miami, Bayside, American Airlines Arena, the
major cruise ships in the Port of Miami, and Miami Beach,
where some of South Florida's most famous residents live.
This helicopter tour is equipped with a headset for every
passenger and air conditioning. The Pilot provides play-
by-play experience. FAA Certified.

MIAMI NICE TOURS
305 949-9180
www.miami-nice.com **WEBSITE DOWN AT
PRESSTIME**

This company offers tours, packages, hotels, transfers and charters. Comprehensive city tours are offered in English, German, French, Italian and Spanish. They also provide airport transfers and charters on luxury buses. They have provided great service since 1987, and all major Internet travel sites work with them. See the best of Florida during one of their daily tours to the Everglades, Key West and Orlando. No group is too big or too small. The company also offers great deals on three- to five-star hotel specials included with a tour and transportation.

MIAMI SEAPLANE TOURS
3401 Rickenbacker Causeway, Key Biscayne-305 361-3909
www.miamiseaplane.com
Experience the thrill and romance of skipping across the wave tops as the seaplane becomes airborne, unveiling the magical city skyline beneath. Choose seaplane tours from 30 minutes to two hours. Reservation required with 24 hours notice.

MIAMI SEAQUARIUM
4400 Rickenbacker Causeway, Virginia Key: 305-361-5705 / www.miamiseaquarium.com
Located on the causeway road to Key Biscayne. A 38-acre tropical paradise with spectacular skyline views of downtown Miami, this is the center of the action if you want to swim with the dolphins, or as they now call it, "dolphin interaction." The dolphins walk on water and killer whales fly through the air. Sea lions delight children of all ages and endangered sea turtles and manatees live here. Enjoy a world-class marine-life entertainment park with eight different marine animal shows and astonishing daily presentations.

MONKEY JUNGLE
14805 SW 216 St., South Miami: 305-235-1611
www.monkeyjungle.com
When Joseph DuMond, an inquisitive animal behaviorist, released six monkeys into the wilds of a dense South Florida hammock in 1933, he didn't realize his endeavors would help shape the attitudes of many in the primatological and zoological fields. The release fifty years ago of that small Java troop signified the beginning of the larger thriving troop that runs free here at Monkey Jungle today.

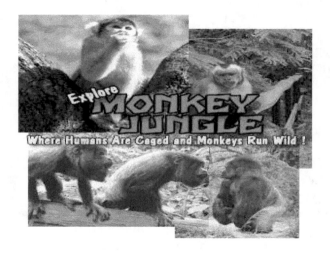

JUNGLE ISLAND
Watson Island: 305-400-7000
www.jungleisland.com
On the island in Biscayne Bay between Miami and South Beach along the MacArthur Causeway. Birds, mammals, primates, fish.

SCHNEBLY REDLAND'S WINERY
30205 SW 217th Ave., Homestead: 305-242-1224

www.schneblywinery.com

This winery in the Redland tropical countryside offers tours and wine tastings around natural coral waterfalls surrounded by lush tropical foliage. Visitors can compare the taste of lychee, passion fruit, carambola, guava and mango wines, just to name a few. This is the southernmost winery in the Continental U.S., handcrafting tropical wines without using grapes. The Grand Tasting Room has a Southern plantation agricultural style. The building is 5,000 square feet and has a view of the tropical courtyard, waterfalls, winery and Grand Tiki, Waterfall Tiki and more than 20,000 square feet of connecting Tikis. They host weddings and corporate retreats. Buses are welcome.

TRAVEL TRACKERS INC.
305 205-0219
www.traveltrackers.com

This full-service USA travel, convention, event and meeting receptive company provides the tri-county area with concierge services and custom tours of Miami, the Everglades, Orlando and the Florida Keys for corporate groups and individuals. They arrange private transportation with bilingual meet-and-greet services at airports, seaports and hotels. A website brochure is available online or mailed on request.

VENETIAN POOL

2701 De Soto Blvd., Coral Gables, 305-460-5306
www.coralgables.com
A Venetian-style lagoon carved out of coral rock, this
historic landmark and swimming pool features caves,
stone bridges and waterfalls. Operates year-round. Call for
information on rates and hours of operation. Children must
be 38 inches tall or show proof that they are 3 years old.
Open 7 days a week from Memorial Day through Labor
Day, closed Mondays during the rest of the year.

VIZCAYA MUSEUM & GARDENS
3251 S. Miami Ave., Miami: 305-250-9133
www.vizcaya.org
Built by agricultural industrialist James Deering in 1916,
Vizcaya Museum & Gardens features a main house, ten
acres of formal gardens, a hardwood hammock, and soon-
to-be-restored historic village. (We think this is one of the
best things to do in the whole County.)

YACHT BRASIL MOTORBOATS & CHARTERS
300 Alton Rd., Suite 108, Miami Beach: 305-722-7200
www.yachtbrasilusa.com
This company offers a fleet of vessels for cruising pleasure
in Miami and around South Florida. They offer half-day
charters, full-day charters, as well as term (week or longer)
charters. They can also accommodate groups up to 400
passengers on larger vessels they work with.

ZOO MIAMI
12400 SW 152nd St., Miami - 305 251-0400
www.zoomiami.org
A wonderful place, but sadly in the middle of Nowhere.
It's only convenient if you're on your way to Key West or
the Federal Prison located right next door. (This is where
they kept Noriega.) Best to just plan a day trip here,
because it'll take half the day to get there and back,
depending on traffic. Their web site has all the pertinent
information.   Rated one of the top 10 zoos in the U.S.
by Tripadvisor.com in 2008, this 340-acre zoo showcases
more than 2,000 animals including koalas, flamingos and
elephants in large open-air exhibits. Things to do and see
include: the 27-acre Amazon and Beyond, American
Banker's Family Aviary, Dr. Wilde's World, Samburu
Giraffe Feeding Station, Humpy's Camel Rides, Nick Jr.'s
favorite animal rescuer Diego, and zookeeper talks

throughout the day. Rent a Safari Cycle, ride the monorail or take a guided tram tour to see the zoo. Picnic and party facilities are available. Open daily 9:30 a.m.-5:30 p.m. (ticket booths close at 4 p.m.). Admission: Adults (age 13 & up) $15.95, children (ages 3-12) $11.95, plus tax. Visit their website for an online admission coupon at the bottom of the Visit the Zoo page.

Chapter 6
SHOPPING & SERVICES

Miami has some excellent shopping opportunities. For high-end shopping, you have Bal Harbour where all the brands you'd find in London, Paris or New York have impressive satellite shops. Then there's everywhere else...

This section is divided into 3 parts: **Bal Harbour**; **South Beach** (with breakdown listings for Ocean Drive, Washington & Collins, Lincoln Road, Espanola Way; and **Mainland Shopping** (with short descriptions of the major shopping areas).

BAL HARBOUR

Most *serious* shoppers make the fifteen-minute drive north of South Beach to 96th Street on Collins Avenue where they can feel enormous comfort perusing the extensive (and expensive) wares at the Miami outposts of such notable names as Cartier, Bulgari, Harry Winston, Armani, Brioni, Bruno Cucinelli, Chanel, Dior, D&G, Pucci, Ferragamo, Graff, Jimmy Choo, Ralph Lauren, Tiffany and the like.

Anchored by Saks and Neiman's (till Neiman's went bankrupt), Bal Harbour Shops is still the place to go. Thankfully, it's concealed from the hoi polloi by tall thick walls. They even charge you for parking, which helps to keep the riff-raff out. (These people were the first ever to charge for parking in a mall.)

But, even if you're not in the mood to buy, it's still fun to stroll through the meticulously landscaped open-air tropical courtyard the Whitman family has created for your enjoyment while you shop. The grounds are rigorously maintained. Flawlessly. It's just a splendid way to spend the afternoon. My niece

Sophie lives just behind Neiman's in Bal Harbour Village. There's a little locked gate she can slip through to meet me there when I make the trek north for lunch at the French bistro Le Zoo. (The steak tartare is not as good as Joe Allen's used to be, believe it or not, but the French fries are skinny, crisp, piping hot and delish. Add a bottle of Sancerre or Brouilly and what more could one want?)

The fountains here are loud, lush and wonderful. Nowhere else in Miami will you find fountains gushing, rushing and slushing so dramatically. If water is money, they throw it away for your pleasure here in Bal Harbour. I look at those sad little fountains on Lincoln Road and think of one word: *pathetic*. To hear the tiny little sprinkling sounds they make reminds you some bum peeing in an alley. (If you don't believe me, go into one of the alleys on South Beach at three in the morning and you can hear this sound for yourself.)

SOUTH BEACH
Ocean Drive
Washington & Collins
Lincoln Road
Espanola Way

OCEAN DRIVE
You can totally forget touristy Ocean Drive (in terms of shopping). But for a certain kind of tourist, Ocean Drive is a favorite, and hanging out at one of the

bumper-to-bumper cafés on South Beach's most famous street sipping gigantic cocktails while watching the parade of people is mandatory. **Mango's** is one spot that is either the apogee (or the nadir, depending on your view) of what it means to be on Ocean Drive. All the servers perform. The **Clevelander** is like a college frat party on Spring Break where no one ever went back to school. But shopping, no. Just the usual low-end but high-priced touristy stuff you'd expect.

<u>WASHINGTON AVENUE & COLLINS AVENUE</u>

The other main street on South Beach is Washington Avenue, which runs parallel to Collins Avenue. I'm convinced whatever poor people are left on South Beach (and there are more than you think) do nothing all day but walk up and down Washington Avenue, making it look worse than it already is. Washington Avenue may be the slummiest street on South Beach, but there's no mistaking its funky allure.

Art Deco fans should take note of the **Art Deco Post Office** and the **Wolfsonian Museum** (filled with lots of examples of Art Deco, it also has a wonderful café and bookstore). The **Wilzig Erotic Art Museum** (an amazing collection of erotic art from around the globe) is a must-see for fans of erotica and the unusual.

My "best finds" on these two streets:

DIESEL
933 Lincoln Rd., 786-718-1555

www.diesel.com
Strictly European in its designs, this store offers a variety of designer jeans, shirts, and accessories.

HELIUM / 760 Ocean Dr. / 305-538-4111. Drop in at this charming little classy gift shop tucked away around the corner.

ARMANI EXCHANGE / 760 Collins Ave. / 305-531-5900
www.armaniexchange.com
Here you'll find Armani's more affordable line including jeans, t-shirts and watches.

GIROUX / 638 Collins Ave. / 305-672-3015. This is the hottest shoe store in town, featuring their own designs (shoes, handbags, belts), but also with names like Michael Kors.

THE WEBSTER
1220 Collins Ave. / 305-674-7899
https://thewebster.us/
The Webster is a 20,000 square feet high luxury multi-brand fashion store. It is located in the heart of Miami Beach in a historic Art Deco building designed in 1939 by famed architect Henry Hohauser. The three-level store is devoted to fashion (men's and women's ready-to-wear and luxury accessories such as shoes, bags, jewelry and watches), photography and entertainment. It's crammed with vintage watches from Rolex, Patek Philippe, Breitling, Cartier, and Longines, and clothing from Marc Jacobs, Givenchy,

Tom Ford, Lanvin, Neil Barrett, Trussardi 1911, and
Adam Kimmel, plus lots more.

URBAN OUTFITTERS
841 Lincoln Rd., 305-534-5166
www.urbanoutfitters.com
Direct from NYC with a South Beach twist, here
you'll find two floors of the funkiest and trendiest
fashions as well as some of the coolest toys, books,
and accessories for your apartment (shag rugs, lamps,
mobiles, and even shower curtains).

LINCOLN ROAD SHOPPING DISTRICT

Collins Avenue to Bay Road, between 16th and 17th
streets (and the Bay to the ocean), Miami Beach: 305
672-1270. http://www.shoponmiamibeach.com
Lincoln Road is a pedestrian mall that
traverses the island east to west from the ocean to the
Bay. It is a shopping, dining and cultural center
featuring unique shops, galleries and restaurants with
indoor and outdoor seating—perfect for people
watching.
Unfortunately, a lot of chains have encroached on
Lincoln Road as national brands with deep pockets
install stores for "branding" purposes and landlords
hike the rents. All this homogenizes the Road, giving
it less character. But there are some good spots. Take
a walk and discover them.
Lincoln Road is a people-watchers' dream and
shopper's paradise, filled with sidewalk cafes (most
of them terribly crappy tourist traps with poor food)

and an amazing variety of boutiques. So you find
name stores like **Gap, Victoria's Secret, Bebe,
French Connection, Guess, Swatch, Diesel** and
Steve Madden. But even if you're not shopping, you
can enjoy a heady view of Art Deco architecture.
Note the Sterling Building in the middle of the Road
(just off the cross street of Michigan Avenue).

7 FOR ALL MANKIND
1008 Lincoln Rd., Miami Beach: 305-538-7355
www.7forallmankind.com
Born in L.A. in the fall of 2000, this store changed the
landscape of premium denim offerings. You can get
"selvage" denim here, a term derived from "self-
edge," which refers to uncut edges that occur when
shuttle looms weave a continuous thread down the
length of the fabric. Men, women and kids, in all
styles.

ALCHEMIST
1109 Lincoln Rd., Miami Beach: 305-531-4653
1111 Lincoln Rd., carpark Level 5, Miami Beach:
305-531-4815
www.shopalchemist.com
The striking design of this store is by Rene Gonzalez.
The layered white squared-off arches with recessed
lighting are visually stunning. Givenchy dresses,
other haute labels like Rick Owens, Martin Margiela.
You've got to visit the store on the fifth floor of the
Herzog & de Meuron parking garage at 1111 Lincoln
Road. Go up for the view and have a look at their
high-end duds. This place is refreshingly European

and a welcome respite from all the crappy tourist traps on South Beach.

ALLSAINTS
910 Lincoln Rd., Miami Beach: 786-517-8181
www.us.allsaints.com
Wide array of apparel for men and women: coats, leather, sweaters, boots and shoes, accessories, bags. The jeans here can be edgy, part retro hippie, part rock n roll. Jeans with metallic highlights are popular, with rises ranging from low-waist to drop-crotch. Polos, sweatshirts, T-shirts.

BRITTO CENTRAL
1102 Lincoln Rd. / 305-531-8821, www.britto.com
Gallery of local artist **Romero Britto** which includes exhibitions of his colorful art plus a gift shop (for those who can't afford the real "art") that includes calendars, mugs, watches, posters and other such tacky trash that's just as ugly and repulsive as his expensive crap.

DECO DRIVE CIGARS
1446 Ocean Dr., 305-672-9032
1650 Meridian Ave., 305-674-1811
414 Lincoln Rd., 305-531-8388
www.decodrivecigars.com
Hey, you can't come to Miami without buying cigars to take home. Here's the best place on South Beach offering the finest selection of cigars and smoking accessories.

THE DOG BAR, 1627 Euclid Ave./ 305-532-5654/ www.dogbar.com. Pet lovers flock to this unique full service luxury specialty pet supply store that features the latest in dog and cat merchandise. (Just off Lincoln Road.)

DYLAN'S CANDY BAR
801 Lincoln Rd., Miami Beach: 305-531-1988
www.dylanscandybar.com
Ralph Lauren's daughter has carved out a special niche for herself in retail, and it has nothing to do with clothing. She's the Candy Queen of New York, and now has a shop on the very expensive corner of Meridian and Lincoln. Cocktails are served outside on Lincoln Road, but not with booze: a chocolate daiquiri, anyone? They don't just sell some of the world's best candy here; they "curate" it, according to Dylan. Interesting novelty items and some accessories as well.

STEVE MADDEN / 443 Lincoln Rd. / 305-673-9997 / www.stevemadden.com.
Shoes, shoes and more shoes. (Interesting accessories, too.)

ESPANOLA WAY
While the city and other guidebooks call this street a "Spanish village," or a "Mediterranean village," and always call it "quaint" and "charming," it's really just a couple of blocks off Washington Avenue (between Fourteenth and Fifteenth streets). On the east end, the Washington Avenue end, there's a youth hostel and a few tourist-trap eateries, so it's always a bustling

corner. There are several really good restaurants here now. (See chapter on Restaurants.) On the west end you'll find a little creperie, **A La Folie**, that's quite nice, where you can sit out under a few shady trees. I've found a few interesting spots for you to visit, though:

MAINLAND SHOPPING

COCOWALK
3015 Grand Ave., Coconut Grove: 305 444-0777
www.cocowalk.net
This retail center is situated in one of Miami's oldest and most prominent communities. Its opening is probably the single most important thing that killed the Grove as a desirable place to be.

This ghastly place is cluttered with mid to low-level crap like the GAP, Victoria's Secret, FYE Music Store, Maui Nix Surf, Starbucks. In June 2010 it welcomed the Paragon Grove 13 luxury movie theatre. According to their PR department: "Nightly live music and special events are always taking place in this exciting retail and entertainment center."

Well, I'm not so sure about "exciting." The place is incredibly ordinary and even tacky.

MIAMI DESIGN DISTRICT
NE 36th to 42nd streets (between NE 2nd Ave. and N Miami Ave.), Miami: 305-772-7100
www.miamidesigndistrict.net
This is one of Miami's most exciting neighborhoods for design, art and other creative companies. It is right in the heart of the city, just 10 minutes from Downtown Miami and directly across the Causeway from Miami Beach (Tuttle Causeway at 41st Street). Store and showroom listings, events and more are available online or over the phone. Great new places for lunch when you want a break. This area made history in the shopping world in 2012 when Louis Vuitton left the Bal Harbour Shops (horrors!) and decamped to the Design District. Other big names (Gucci, Cartier) have followed and others are expected to come here as leases come up for renewal in Bal Harbour. Construction is currently underway to create a pedestrian friendly street that will mimic Bal Harbour's famous open-air oasis, but it can't really compare. The District now boasts an impressive listing of luxury brands including: **Alchemist, Armani, Balenciaga, Bottega Veneta, Burberry, BVLGARI, Cartier, D&G, Dior, Tom Ford, Christian Louboutin, Fendi, Ferragamo, Gucci,** and **Harry Winston**. The District has become a

melting pot of art, music, shopping, and high-end restaurants like: **Baccarat Boutique B Bar and Lounge, Estefan Kitchen, Harry's Pizzeria, Le Jardinier, MC Kitchen,** and **Michael's Genuine Food & Drink.**

DOWNTOWN MIAMI SHOPPING DISTRICT
Biscayne Boulevard to 2nd Avenue West; SE 1st Street to NE 3rd Street, Miami: 305-379-7070; http://www.downtownmiami.com
Historic Flagler Street is the heart of the City of Miami. Hundreds of stores and shops make up the Downtown Shopping District, anchored by **Macy's Marshalls, Ross Dress for Less,** and **La Epoca** (imported from Havana). Visitors can shop all day, lunch on food from almost anywhere in the world, visit art and historical museums, or just stroll the streets of Miami's historic district. Also the destination for world-class jewelry shopping, including the Seybold Building which boasts more than 280 jewelers. Take the Downtown Miami Partnership historic walking tour every Saturday at 10:30 a.m. Call for reservations.

BAYSIDE MARKETPLACE
401 Biscayne Blvd., Miami: 305-577-3344 www.baysidemarketplace.com
A dining, entertainment and retail complex located on beautiful Biscayne Bay in Downtown Miami. Visitors will find more than 150 shops, restaurants and bars, including national retailers and unique shops, Miami's Hard Rock Cafe, Bubba Gump Shrimp Co., and an "international" food court that's really scary.

Free nightly entertainment at the waterfront Marina stage.

Tour boats offer sightseeing or dance cruises throughout the day. Ideal for group outings and special events. The Marketplace has just added the176-foot tall **Sky Views Miami Wheel** featuring 42 climate-controlled gondolas offering breathtaking panoramic views of downtown Miami and the surrounding area.

MARY BRICKELL VILLAGE

901 S. Miami Ave., Miami: 305-381-6130
www.marybrickellvillage.com
This retail and restaurant destination is right in the center of everything. Tenants include Balans Restaurant, P.F. Chang's, Starbucks and Regions Bank.

DOWNTOWN CORAL GABLES/MIRACLE MILE

220 Miracle Mile, Coral Gables: 305-569-0311
http://www.shopcoralgables.com
When I was a kid, my grandmother used to drag me down here to go with her as she shopped "The Mile." Still features quality shops, art galleries, boutiques, restaurants and a live theater (Actors Playhouse, does top quality work) in a lushly landscaped environment of tree-lined streets. Shoppers will find unique jewelry, apparel, home furnishings, salons and spas, and other specialty shops.

Chapter 7
SPAS

BILTMORE SPA

1200 Anastasia Ave., Coral Gables: 305/913-3187
www.biltmorehotel.com

Located on the seventh floor, with panoramic views
from floor to ceiling windows, this spa's elite
facilities are impressive. Beige and green earth tones,
natural woods and the quiet murmur of falling water
enhance an environment of calm and beauty. The spa
offers a wide selection of therapies and treatments
customized to help guests achieve long-term benefits
and individualized wellness. Their menu includes a
selection of massage therapies, skin care services,

body treatments and wraps, signature couples' treatments, and a full-service hair and nail salon.

GUYAND GIRL SALON & SPA
Mondrian, 1100 West Ave., Miami Beach: 305/514-1950
http://guyandgirlspa.com
This spa features 4,000 square feet of Marcel Wanders-designed interiors with six treatment rooms equipped to offer an extensive variety of services. Along with signature Milk and Honey treatments and private garden-view terrace, the spa is an exclusive carrier of products by SJAL and Butter London.

K'ALMA SPA
1144 Ocean Dr., Miami Beach: 305-534-5555
www.hotelvictorsouthbeach.com
Welcome to the first U.S. Peruvian Crystal Color Therapy Spa located in the Hotel Victor. This 6,000-square-foot oasis of rejuvenation and relaxation embraces ancient traditions of beauty and cleansing within a setting of modern luxury. The spa offers a full range of distinctive European-inspired treatments including Hammam V, the traditional Moroccan practice of cleansing the body with black olive beldi soap, then exfoliating with a Hammam glove, followed by a mask of Moroccan lava clay and hydrating massage.

LAPIS SPA
FONTAINEBLEAU MIAMI BEACH

4441 Collins Ave., Miami Beach: 305/674-4772
www.fontainebleau.com
This two-level spa harnesses the natural qualities of
water to create a shared experience that is both
restorative and renewing. Mineral rich water in many
forms is used throughout the 40,000-square-foot spa
that features 30 private treatment rooms as well as a
co-ed pool and lounge area. Merging age-old
techniques with the latest contemporary technology
and design, this spa provides guests with stress relief,
anti-aging and wellness solutions.

RITZ-CARLTON SPA, KEY BISCAYNE
455 Grand Bay Dr., Key Biscayne: 305/365-4157
www.ritzcarlton.com
An oasis of tropical splendor, this award-winning
20,000-square-foot retreat features a menu with
ocean-inspired natural therapies, an exclusive Prada
beauty line, a dedicated menu of services for
gentlemen, 21 treatment rooms, a Wellness and
Fitness center, relaxation lounges, a private pedicure
suite, a Pilates studio and attentive staff to complete
the spa experience.

STANDARD SPA MIAMI BEACH
40 Island Ave., Miami Beach: 305/673-1717
www.standardhotels.com
This holistic and hydrotherapy-oriented spa hotel is
inspired by global bathing cultures, self-teaching and
healing. Located on the waters of Belle Isle, Miami
Beach, this contemporary spa encourages the
communal, shared rituals of ancient bathing
traditions, with a Turkish-style Hamam, Roman

waterfall, Aroma steam room, Finnish sauna and mud baths.

SPA V
1144 Ocean Dr., Miami Beach: 305-728-6500
www.hotelvictorsouthbeach.com
This 6,000-square-foot oasis of rejuvenation and relaxation embraces ancient traditions of beauty and cleansing within a setting of modern luxury. The spa offers a full range of distinctive European-inspired treatments including Hammam V, the traditional Moroccan practice of cleansing the body with black olive beldi soap, then exfoliating with a Hammam glove, followed by a mask of Moroccan lava clay and hydrating massage. The Melt Me Massage is designed to melt away tension and stress from head to toe.

SPA AT SHORE CLUB
1901 Collins Ave., Miami Beach: 305/695-3292
www.shoreclub.com
This beautiful rooftop retreat is an 8,000-square-foot full-service facility. It features a serene Zen-like atmosphere with teak and warm-toned materials, wet and dry treatment rooms, outdoor terraces and massage decks, and exclusive products. Guests can indulge in magnificent ocean views while rejuvenating their Yin Yang energies and replenishing their natural body rhythms. The spa offers an exclusive selection of massage, facial, body and nail treatments for women and men, available in private suites or outdoor terraces.

THE SPA AT ONE BAL HARBOUR

10295 Collins Ave., Bal Harbour: 305-455-5400
www.ritzcarlton.com
This spa offers five-star delivery of beauty and well-being treatments, including personalized facials, body sublimation, 5-senses hydrotherapy, harmonizing massage, intensive hand and foot therapies and totally transforming day experience packages.

INDEX

T

When was the last time you had a dental check up ?

There is a good way to avoid dentures, pain and extensive dental therapy... it's called prevention and early detection.

Make an appointment today with the dentist that has 42 years of experience, teaches other dentists and wrote the book "Understanding First Class Dental Care".
Save money and your teeth.

Dr. David Vine
cosmetic & restorative dentistry

Call 305-538-1115
www.davidvinedentist.com

The Sheridan Center
400 Arthur Godfrey Rd,
Suite 403
Miami Beach

FREE Valet Parking

218

WANT 3 *FREE* THRILLERS?

Why, of course you do!

If you like these writers--
Vince Flynn, Brad Thor, Tom Clancy, James Patterson,
David Baldacci, John Grisham, Brad Meltzer, Daniel
Silva, Don DeLillo
If you like these TV series –
House of Cards, Scandal, West Wing, The Good Wife,
Madam Secretary, Designated Survivor

You'll love the **unputdownable** series about
Jack's world, with political intrigue, romance, suspense.

Besides writing travel books, I've written political thrillers
for many years that have delighted hundreds of thousands
of readers. I want to introduce you to my work!
Send me an email and I'll send you a link where you can
download the first 3 books in my bestselling series,
absolutely FREE.

Just tell me you're responding to my offer in this book.

andrewdelaplaine@mac.com